ASIA BOND MONITOR
SEPTEMBER 2022

ADB

ASIAN DEVELOPMENT BANK

© 2022 Asian Development Bank
6 ADB Avenue, Mandaluyong City, 1550 Metro Manila, Philippines
Tel +63 2 8632 4444; Fax +63 2 8636 2444
www.adb.org

Some rights reserved. Published in 2022.

ISBN 978-92-9269-734-1 (print); 978-92-9269-735-8 (electronic); 978-92-9269-736-5 (ebook)
ISSN 2219-1518 (print), 2219-1526 (electronic)
Publication Stock No. TCS220379-2
DOI: http://dx.doi.org/10.22617/TCS220379-2

The views expressed in this publication are those of the authors and do not necessarily reflect the views and policies of the Asian Development Bank (ADB) or its Board of Governors or the governments they represent.

ADB does not guarantee the accuracy of the data included in this publication and accepts no responsibility for any consequence of their use. The mention of specific companies or products of manufacturers does not imply that they are endorsed or recommended by ADB in preference to others of a similar nature that are not mentioned.

By making any designation of or reference to a particular territory or geographic area, or by using the term "country" in this document, ADB does not intend to make any judgments as to the legal or other status of any territory or area.

Corrigenda to ADB publications may be found at http://www.adb.org/publications/corrigenda.

Note:
ADB recognizes "China" as the People's Republic of China; "Hong Kong" and "Hongkong" as Hong Kong, China; "Korea" as the Republic of Korea; "Siam" as Thailand; "Vietnam" as Viet Nam; "Russia" as the Russian Federation; "Hanoi" as Ha Noi; and "Saigon" as Ho Chi Minh City.

Cover design by Erickson Mercado.

Contents

Emerging East Asian Local Currency Bond Markets: A Regional Update

Emerging East Asian Local Currency Bond Markets: A Regional Update

Executive Summary

Recent Developments in Emerging East Asian Financial Conditions

Long-term bond yields declined and yield curves flattened in emerging East Asia on a dimming economic outlook.[1] Despite continued inflationary pressure and accelerated monetary tightening, a moderating growth outlook and mounting downside risks contributed to declining yields on 10-year local currency (LCY) government bonds and flattening yield curves, as proxied by narrowing spreads between 10-year and 2-year bond yields between 15 June and 24 August. Regional currencies also collectively depreciated against the United States (US) dollar by an average of 1.8% (simple) and 2.1% (gross-domestic-product-weighted) during the review period. Short-term bond yields rose in a few markets as central banks accelerated monetary tightening to tame inflation and safeguard financial stability.

Financial conditions eased modestly on improved market sentiment, especially since mid-July. From 15 June to 24 August, the region witnessed risk premiums narrowing by an average of 9 basis points (simple) and 11 basis points (gross-domestic-product-weighted), as well as a weighted average gain of 1.8% in all equity markets except the People's Republic of China (PRC) and Hong Kong, China. In August, regional equity markets experienced net portfolio inflows of USD4.2 billion, a reversal from outflows of USD1.8 billion in July. The improvement in financial conditions, especially since the second half of July, was supported by optimism over better-than-expected corporate earnings and expectations of a possible peak in inflation in the US, and thus a milder-than-expected tightening path by the US Federal Reserve.

The risk to the outlook of regional financial conditions is tilted to the downside. Moderating economic growth remains a key short-term risk, together with mounting uncertainties regarding inflationary pressure, the pace of the Federal Reserve's monetary tightening, lingering impacts of the pandemic, potential spillovers from a faster-than-expected slowdown in the PRC, and the possibility of greater-than-expected spillovers from the Russian invasion of Ukraine. Over the medium-term, asset vulnerability associated with high-emitting sectors during their transition to net-zero emissions, and the need to provide sufficient finance to fund low-carbon projects and support the transition of high-emitting projects in a sustainable way, pose new challenges to the financial sector.

Recent Developments in Local Currency Bond Markets in Emerging East Asia

LCY bond markets in emerging East Asia experienced record-high issuance in the second quarter (Q2) of 2022. By the end of June, LCY bonds outstanding in regional markets reached USD22.9 trillion on quarterly issuance of USD2.4 trillion. The sizable issuance was largely driven by increased financing needs from the PRC to stimulate its economy. The PRC accounted for 68.1% of emerging East Asian bond issuance during Q2 2022. Member economies of the Association of Southeast Asian Nations (ASEAN) had outstanding bonds totaling USD2.0 trillion at the end of June, representing 8.6% of all emerging East Asian bonds outstanding. ASEAN members' combined issuance climbed to USD418.1 billion during Q2 2022 on growth of 10.3% quarter-on-quarter (q-o-q), accounting for 17.5% of the region's total issuance during the quarter.

The public sector continued to dominate regional bond markets in Q2 2022. LCY government bonds totaled USD14.5 trillion and comprised 63.1% of emerging East Asia's outstanding LCY bonds at the end of June. During the quarter, LCY government bond issuance tallied USD1.6 trillion, posting q-o-q growth of 25.9% as governments borrowed to support economic recovery. Meanwhile, private sector bond issuance contracted 4.9% q-o-q, with total corporate debt financing of USD812.6 billion, due to the weak economic outlook and rising borrowing costs.

---

[1] Emerging East Asia is defined to include Cambodia; the People's Republic of China; Hong Kong, China; Indonesia; the Republic of Korea; the Lao People's Democratic Republic; Malaysia; the Philippines; Singapore; Thailand; and Viet Nam.

Relatively more shorter-tenor government bonds were issued during Q2 2022. Emerging East Asia's LCY government bond market is largely dominated by medium- to longer-term maturities, with 55.2% of outstanding government bonds at the end of June carrying a maturity of over 5 years. During Q2 2022, however, 50.5% of government bond issuance carried a tenor of 5 years or less, and the share of government bonds with tenors of 1–3 years climbed to 33.4% of total issuance from 25.9% in the previous quarter, reflecting increased financing needs over the short and medium terms.

A softened economic outlook dented investment appetite in the ASEAN+3 sustainable bond market in Q2 2022. However, the market still expanded to a size of USD503.5 billion at the end of June on issuance of USD61.0 billion, which reflected a 5.2% q-o-q contraction. The amount of ASEAN+3 sustainable bonds outstanding as a share of the global market slid to 15.3% at the end of June from 16.7% in March. While the private sector dominated issuances of sustainable bonds in the region, the negative economic outlook led the public sector's share to rise to 11.0% at the end of June from 9.8% at the end of March. The term structure of the region's sustainable bond market remained focused on short and medium tenors, with a size-weighted average tenor of 4.3 years for outstanding bonds at the end of Q2 2022 and 4.6 years for bonds issued during the quarter.

Global and Regional Market Developments

Long-term bond yields declined and yield curves flattened in emerging East Asia on a dimming economic outlook.

Between 15 June and 24 August, a moderating growth outlook and mounting downside risks in emerging East Asia contributed to declining yields for 10-year local currency (LCY) government bonds, flattened yield curves, and currency depreciations against the United States (US) dollar across the region.[1] Short-term bond yield rose in a few markets as central banks accelerated monetary tightening to tame inflation and safeguard financial stability. Meanwhile, financial conditions eased modestly, as evidenced by narrowed risk premiums, and equities rallied in most emerging East Asian markets, largely supported by optimistic market sentiment since the second half of July on better-than-expected corporate earnings and expectations of a possible peak in inflation

and thus a milder-than-expected tightening path by the US Federal Reserve (**Table A**).

From 15 June to 24 August, 10-year government bond yields trended downward and yield curves flattened, as proxied by narrowed spreads between 10-year and 2-year bond yields in most major advanced economies, driven by a weakening economic outlook.

In the US, growth prospects have dimmed, inflation remains elevated, and the Federal Reserve continues with aggressive tightening. During the review period, however, market sentiments in global financial markets were hugely shaped by expectations based on US economic data releases and forward guidance from the Federal Reserve. Tightening financial conditions were exacerbated on 13 July when US consumer price inflation for the month of June posted a 41-year high of

Table A: Changes in Global Financial Condition in Emerging East Asia and Major Advanced Economies

	2-Year Government Bond (bps)	10-Year Government Bond (bps)	5-Year Credit Default Swap Spread (bps)	Equity Index (%)	FX Rate (%)
Major Advanced Economies					
United States	20	(18)	–	9.3	–
United Kingdom	97	23	6	2.7	(3.1)
Japan	(6)	(3)	(2)	6.0	(2.4)
Germany	(16)	(27)	4	(2.0)	(4.6)
Emerging East Asia					
China, People's Rep. of	(18)	(19)	(11)	(2.7)	(2.1)
Hong Kong, China	8	(43)	–	(9.6)	0.04
Indonesia	44	(39)	(13)	2.7	(0.7)
Korea, Rep. of	(21)	(33)	(16)	0.003	(3.9)
Malaysia	(13)	(37)	(13)	0.6	(1.6)
Philippines	20	(101)	(12)	5.1	(4.7)
Singapore	0	(37)	–	4.1	(0.6)
Thailand	(30)	(53)	2	2.4	(2.8)
Viet Nam	93	22	(2)	5.2	(1.0)

( ) = negative, – = not available, bps = basis points, FX = foreign exchange.
Notes:
1. Data reflect changes between 15 June 2022 and 24 August 2022.
2. A positive (negative) value for the FX rate indicates the appreciation (depreciation) of the local currency against the United States dollar.
Source: *AsianBondsOnline* computations based on Bloomberg LP data.

---

[1] Emerging East Asia is defined to include Cambodia; the People's Republic of China; Hong Kong, China; Indonesia; the Republic of Korea; the Lao People's Democratic Republic; Malaysia; the Philippines; Singapore; Thailand; and Viet Nam.

9.1% year-on-year (y-o-y), as the market showed concern that the Federal Reserve would become even more aggressive in its monetary tightening—an 80% probability emerged of a 100 basis points (bps) hike at the 27–28 July Federal Open Market Committee (FOMC) meeting. Such fears quickly waned as both Federal Reserve Governor Christopher Waller, on 14 July, and St. Louis Federal Reserve President James Bullard, on 15 July, indicated their support for a 75 bps rate hike at the July meeting as previously anticipated.

Beginning in mid-July, investors expressed optimism over an expected "Fed pivot," or milder-than-expected tightening by the Federal Reserve, supported by a smaller contraction in US gross domestic product (GDP) in the second quarter (Q2) of 2022 compared with the previous quarter, better-than-expected corporate earnings, slightly lower inflation in July, as well as a continued strong domestic job market. Per data released on 28 July, US GDP contracted an annualized 0.9% in Q2 2022 (later revised to -0.6% on 25 August), which was less than the 1.6% contraction in the first quarter (Q1) of 2022. On 5 August, US nonfarm payrolls showed a gain of 528,000 in July, up from 398,000 in June, while the July unemployment rate fell further to 3.5% after holding steady at 3.6% from March to June. Furthermore, the release of July consumer price inflation of 8.5% y-o-y on 10 August ignited expectations of a possible peak in inflation. US producer price inflation also retreated from 11.1% y-o-y in May and 11.3% y-o-y in June to 9.8% y-o-y in July. These data contributed to optimistic sentiment in the market and some speculation on the possibility of less significant monetary tightening by the Federal Reserve.

In contrast to expectations of a pivot, the Federal Reserve repeatedly affirmed it would continue with its tightening trajectory to tame inflation. During the July FOMC meeting, Federal Reserve Chairman Jerome Powell noted that market expectations of the path of the future federal funds rate were lower than what the Federal Reserve had indicated in its June dot-plot. Moreover, during the Aspen Ideas Conference on 10 August, Minneapolis Federal Reserve Bank President Neel Kashkari said that he did not see the need for any deviation from the current trajectory. The San Francisco Federal Reserve Bank's Mary Daly, in an interview with the *Financial Times* on 11 August, said that it was still too early to assume that inflation is on its way to being contained. St. Louis Federal Reserve President James Bullard, in a *Wall Street Journal* interview

on 18 August, indicated support for a 75 bps rate hike in September as he was also not ready to say that inflation had peaked. Meanwhile, the Federal Reserve also confirmed its commitment to continue reducing its bond holdings. Amid such developments, on 24 August the federal funds futures market priced in a slightly lower chance for a 50 bps (45.5%), compared to a 75 bps (54.5%), rate hike at the September FOMC meeting. Expectations for a 75 bps rate hike at the September meeting were further strengthened by Federal Reserve Chairman Jerome Powell's speech at the Jackson Hole conference on 26 August, which highlighted that "reducing inflation is likely to require a sustained period of below-trend growth." Powell also said that the Federal Reserve's policy stance would be sufficiently restrictive to return inflation to its 2.0% target, which increased the chance for a 75 bps hike in September, as implied in the federal funds futures market, to 61.0% on the same day.

The euro area continued to grapple with both high inflation and growth moderation. In July, inflation in the euro area rose to 8.9% y-o-y from 8.6% y-o-y in June and 8.1% y-o-y in May. Inflation rose further to 9.1% y-o-y in August. Meanwhile, GDP growth softened to 3.9% y-o-y in Q2 2022 from 5.4% y-o-y in Q1 2022. The European Central Bank (ECB) noted that uncertainties related to the Russian invasion of Ukraine have led to a weakening of economic growth as well as a rise in food and energy prices. As inflationary pressure remained elevated, the ECB raised its key policy rates—the refinancing rate, marginal lending facility, and deposit facility—by 50 bps each to 0.50%, 0.75%, and 0.0%, respectively, during its 21 July policy meeting. The rate hikes were larger than the 25 bps rate hikes previously signaled by the ECB. To ensure the smooth and effective transmission of its monetary stance, the ECB unveiled the Transmission Protection Instrument, which allows the central bank to purchase securities issued by the governments and government agencies of individual member countries based on their current financial conditions.

In Japan, inflation rose modestly compared to the US and euro area, while its economic outlook weakened too. In July, the Bank of Japan (BOJ) revised downward its GDP forecast for 2022 from 2.9% made in April to 2.4%, while raising its inflation forecast for 2022 to 2.3% from the forecast of 1.9% made in April. While inflation in Japan stayed above the BOJ's 2.0% target, recording 2.5% y-o-y in both April and May, as well as 2.4% y-o-y in June and 2.6% y-o-y in July, it is much milder compared to that in the US and euro area. Meanwhile, Japan's GDP posted annualized growth of 3.5% in Q2 2022 versus 0.2% in Q1 2022. With this development, the BOJ maintained its monetary policy during its 21 July meeting, keeping the short-term policy rate target at −0.1% and the 10-year Japan Government Bond yield target at 0.0%, and leaving unchanged the amount of monthly asset purchases of exchange-traded funds and Japanese real investment trusts.

Nearly all 10-year local currency government bond yields fell in emerging East Asian economies and yield curves flattened between 15 July and 24 August, largely driven by the softened growth outlook in the region. In emerging East Asia, higher global oil and food prices, lingering supply chain disruptions, and economic re-openings contributed to rising inflation (**Figure A**). Regional central banks have accelerated monetary tightening, via more and larger rate hikes, to ease inflationary pressure and safeguard financial stability amid aggressive Federal Reserve tightening (**Table B**). From 1 April to 15 June, emerging East Asia witnessed four 25 bps rate hikes, while from 15 June to 25 August, emerging East Asian economies conducted eight rate hikes with an average hike of 38 bps. Accelerated monetary tightening in the region pushed up 2-year bond yields in

some markets, while a moderation in the regional growth outlook led to lower 10-year bond yields and flattened yield curves, as proxied by narrowed spreads between 10-year bond yields over 2-year bond yields.

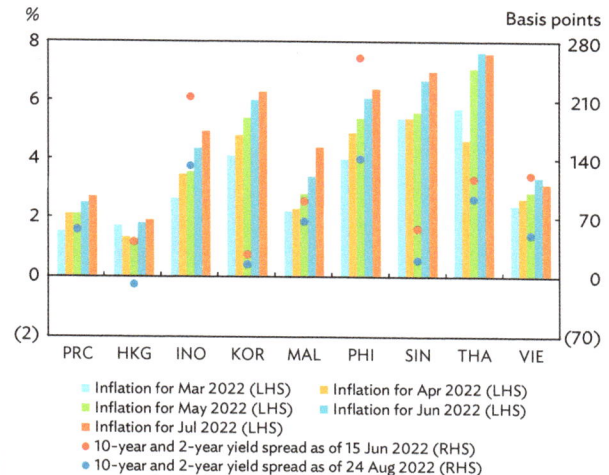

Figure A: Inflation and Changes in Term Spreads in Emerging East Asia

Inflation for Mar 2022 (LHS)   Inflation for Apr 2022 (LHS)
Inflation for May 2022 (LHS)   Inflation for Jun 2022 (LHS)
Inflation for Jul 2022 (LHS)
10-year and 2-year yield spread as of 15 Jun 2022 (RHS)
10-year and 2-year yield spread as of 24 Aug 2022 (RHS)

( ) = negative; PRC = China, People's Rep. of; HKG = Hong Kong, China; INO = Indonesia; KOR = Korea, Rep. of; LHS = left-hand side; MAL = Malaysia; PHI = Philippines; RHS = right-hand side; SIN = Singapore; THA = Thailand; VIE = Viet Nam.
Sources: Various local sources.

Table B: Changes in Monetary Stances in Major Advanced Economies and Emerging East Asia

Economy	Policy Rate 15-Aug-2021 (%)	Aug-2021	Sep-2021	Oct-2021	Nov-2021	Dec-2021	Jan-2022	Feb-2022	Mar-2022	Apr-2022	May-2022	Jun-2022	Jul-2022	Aug-2022	Policy Rate 25-Aug-2022 (%)	Change in Policy Rate (basis points)
United States	0.25								↑0.25		↑0.50	↑0.75	↑0.75		2.50	↑225
Euro Area	(0.50)												↑0.50		0.00	↑50
United Kingdom	0.10					↑0.15		↑0.25	↑0.25		↑0.25	↑0.25		↑0.50	1.75	↑165
Japan	(0.10)														(0.10)	
China, People's Rep. of	2.95						↓0.10							↓0.10	2.75	↓20
Indonesia	3.50													↑0.25	3.75	↑25
Korea, Rep. of	0.50	↑0.25			↑0.25		↑0.25			↑0.25	↑0.25		↑0.50	↑0.25	2.50	↑200
Malaysia	1.75										↑0.25		↑0.25		2.25	↑50
Philippines	2.00										↑0.25	↑0.25	↑0.75	↑0.50	3.75	↑175
Singapore	–		↑				↑			↑			↑		–	–
Thailand	0.50													↑0.25	0.75	↑25
Viet Nam	4.00														4.00	

( ) = negative.
Notes:
1. Data coverage is from 15 August 2021 to 25 August 2022.
2. For the People's Republic of China, data used in the chart are for the 1-year medium-term lending facility rate. While the 1-year benchmark lending rate is the official policy rate of the People's Bank of China, market players use the 1-year medium-term lending facility rate as a guide for the monetary policy direction of the People's Bank of China.
3. The up (down) arrow for Singapore signifies monetary policy tightening (loosening) by its central bank. Monetary Authority of Singapore utilizes the exchange rate to guide its monetary policy.
Sources: Various central bank websites.

Viet Nam is the only market in emerging East Asia that witnessed a rise in both the 2-year and 10-year yields. The overall uptick in bond yields was partly driven by the State Bank of Vietnam's money market operations to tighten liquidity and stabilize the Vietnamese dong, although the central bank did not directly adjust the policy rate. Meanwhile, the central bank increased the issuance of central bank bills in Q2 2022, draining liquidity and indirectly pushing up bond yields.

Indonesia witnessed a 44 bps increase in its 2-year yield, largely driven by an unexpected policy rate hike by Bank Indonesia of 25 bps on 23 August. Prior to the rate hike, Bank Indonesia used open market operations to tighten liquidity conditions and lift yields, particularly for the 2-week and 1-year maturities. It also started to offload bonds with maturities of up to 5 years from its balance sheet under its burden-sharing agreement with the government during the pandemic.

The Philippines saw an increase in its 2-year bond yield during the review period as the Bangko Sentral ng Pilipinas has been one of the most aggressive in the region, hiking the policy rate by a total of 175 bps with four consecutive monthly rate hikes from May through August to contain inflation.

Bucking the monetary tightening trend in the region, the People's Bank of China eased its monetary stance by lowering the 7-day repo rate and 1-year medium-term lending facility rate by 10 bps each on 15 August. On 22 August, it cut the 5-year loan prime rate and 1-year loan prime rate by 15 bps and 5 bps, respectively, to support recovery and stabilize the real estate sector as growth was negatively affected by measures to contain the pandemic. Meanwhile, inflation in the People's Republic of China (PRC) remained modest compared to other regional economies, offering some policy scope. With a subdued economic outlook and easing monetary stances, both the 2-year and 10-year yields declined in the PRC.

Rising inflation and a moderation in the regional growth outlook contributed to currency depreciations across the region between 15 June and 24 August. From 15 June to 15 July, regional foreign exchange rates posted a simple average loss of 1.7% (or 1.0% in GDP-weighted average terms) against a strong US dollar that was buttressed by aggressive Federal Reserve tightening. The currency depreciations continued from 15 July to 24 August by a

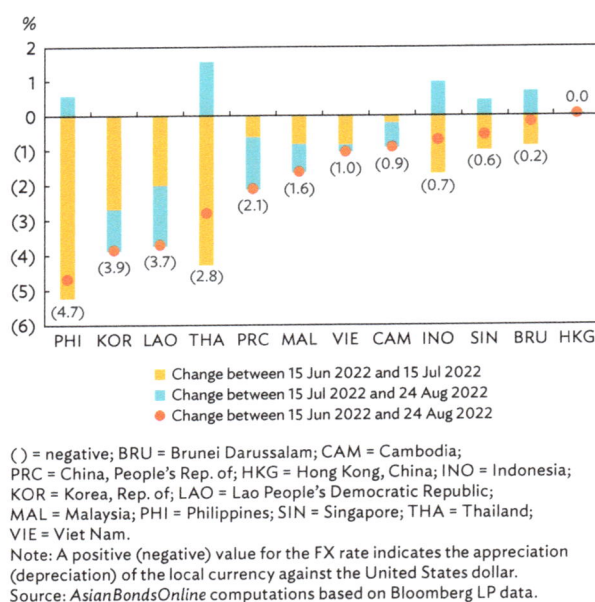

Figure B: Changes in Emerging East Asian Currencies

( ) = negative; BRU = Brunei Darussalam; CAM = Cambodia; PRC = China, People's Rep. of; HKG = Hong Kong, China; INO = Indonesia; KOR = Korea, Rep. of; LAO = Lao People's Democratic Republic; MAL = Malaysia; PHI = Philippines; SIN = Singapore; THA = Thailand; VIE = Viet Nam.
Note: A positive (negative) value for the FX rate indicates the appreciation (depreciation) of the local currency against the United States dollar.
Source: *AsianBondsOnline* computations based on Bloomberg LP data.

simple average of 0.2% (or 1.1% in GDP-weighted average terms), although improved market sentiment supported currencies in a few markets (**Figure B**). The Philippines witnessed the region's largest depreciation versus the US dollar during the review period on a widened trade deficit and consecutive monthly outflows from the equity market since March.

Despite a weakening economic outlook, optimistic market sentiment fueled by expectations of a potential Fed pivot led to a rally in equity markets, narrowed risk premiums, and capital inflows into the region beginning in mid-July.

During the review period, equity markets in the region, excluding the PRC and Hong Kong, China, collectively gained after fears of a 100 bps rate hike by the Federal Reserve in July were cooled by forward guidance from two Federal Reserve officials on 14–15 July (**Figure C**). From 15 June to 15 July, nearly all emerging East Asian equity markets posted losses amid a weak global economic outlook and aggressive Federal Reserve tightening, generating a market-weighted average loss of 3.1% across the region. As market sentiment improved after 15 July, most regional markets rallied. From 15 July to 24 August, regional equity markets, excluding the PRC and Hong Kong, China, all gained, posting a value-weighted return of 5.6%. From 15 June to 24 August, equity markets in the PRC and

Figure C: Movements in Equity Indexes in Emerging East Asia

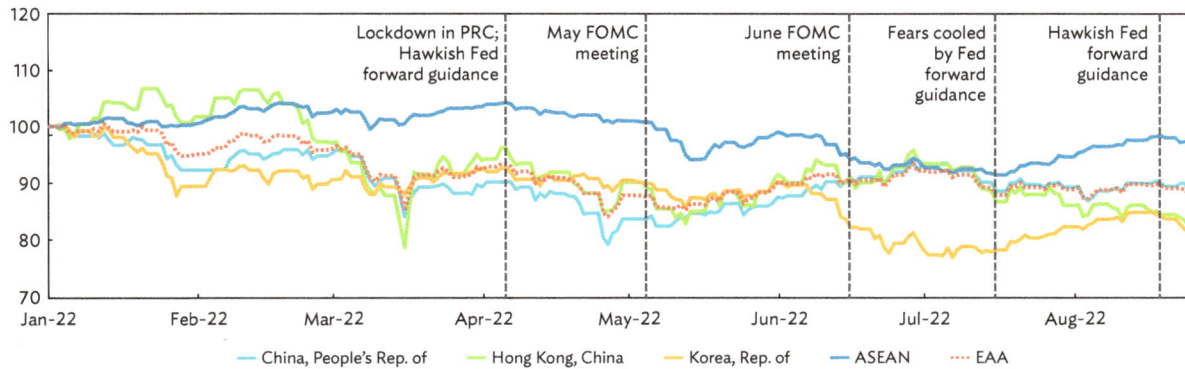

ASEAN = Association of Southeast Asian Nations, bps = basis points, EEA = European Economic Area, Fed = Federal Reserve, FOMC = Federal Open Market Committee, PRC = People's Republic of China.
Notes:
1. 1 January 2022 = 100.
2. ASEAN comprises the markets of Indonesia, Malaysia, the Philippines, Singapore, Thailand, and Viet Nam.
3. Data as of 24 August 2022.
Source: *AsianBondsOnline* computations based on Bloomberg LP data.

Hong Kong, China recorded losses of 2.7% and 9.6%, respectively, over concerns about a slowdown in the PRC's economic growth. The PRC's GDP grew only 0.4% y-o-y in Q2 2022, after gaining 4.8% y-o-y in the previous quarter, as economic activities were negatively affected by measures to contain the coronavirus disease (COVID-19) pandemic. Hong Kong, China was the sole market in the region to post two consecutive quarterly GDP contractions of 3.9% y-o-y and 1.3% y-o-y in Q1 2022 and Q2 2022, respectively.

Similarly, improved sentiment since mid-July drove down risk premiums, proxied by credit default swap spreads, across the region. From 15 June to 15 July, risk premiums in major regional economies collectively widened by an average of 21 bps (simple average) and 9 bps (GDP-weighted) on tightening global monetary stances and a gloomy recovery outlook, but the trend reversed between 15 July and 24 August when risk premiums collectively narrowed by an average of 30 bps (simple average) and 20 bps (GDP-weighted). From 15 June to 24 August, risk premiums in the region narrowed by 9 bps in simple average terms and 11 bps in GDP-weighted average terms (**Figure D**).

Improved market sentiment brought portfolio inflows back into regional equity markets in August. The region experienced net inflows of USD7.0 billion in equity markets from 1 June to 24 August (**Figure E**). The gains

Figure D: Changes in Credit Default Swap Spreads in Emerging East Asia (senior 5-year)

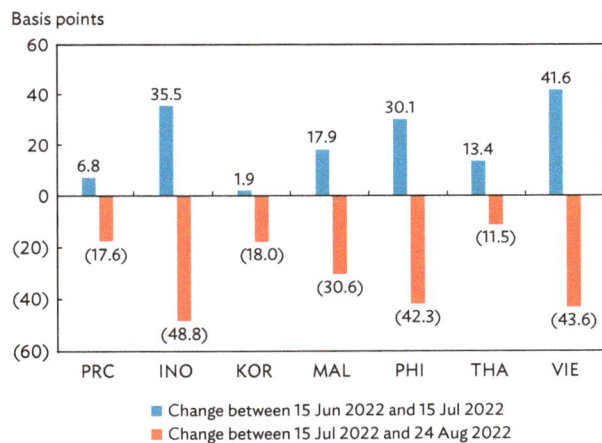

( ) = negative; PRC = China, People's Rep. of; INO = Indonesia; KOR = Korea, Rep. of; MAL = Malaysia; PHI = Philippines; THA = Thailand; VIE = Viet Nam.
Source: *AsianBondsOnline* computations based on Bloomberg LP data.

stemmed largely from the PRC, especially in June, when USD10.9 billion of inflows were recorded following the introduction of economic stimulus measures and the lifting of a COVID-19 lockdown in Shanghai. However, the gloomy economic outlook led to outflows from the PRC's equity market in July. Excluding the PRC, the region witnessed net outflows of USD1.0 billion from 1 June to 24 August; in June, outflows of USD6.3 billion

Figure E: Foreign Capital Flows into Equity Markets in Emerging East Asia

USD billion

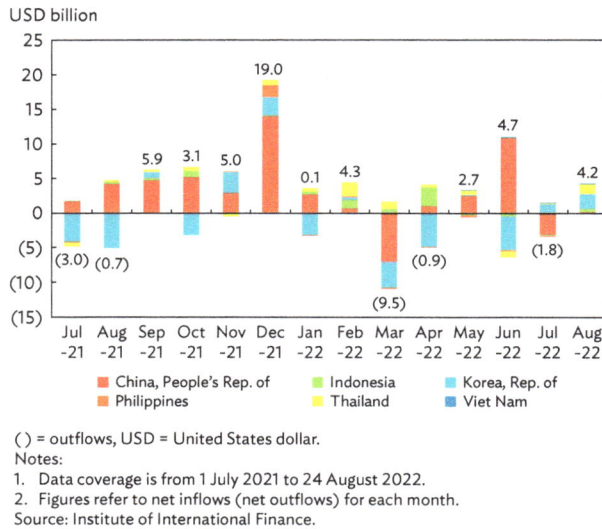

( ) = outflows, USD = United States dollar.
Notes:
1. Data coverage is from 1 July 2021 to 24 August 2022.
2. Figures refer to net inflows (net outflows) for each month.
Source: Institute of International Finance.

Figure F: Foreign Capital Flows in Local Currency Bond Markets in Emerging East Asia

USD billion

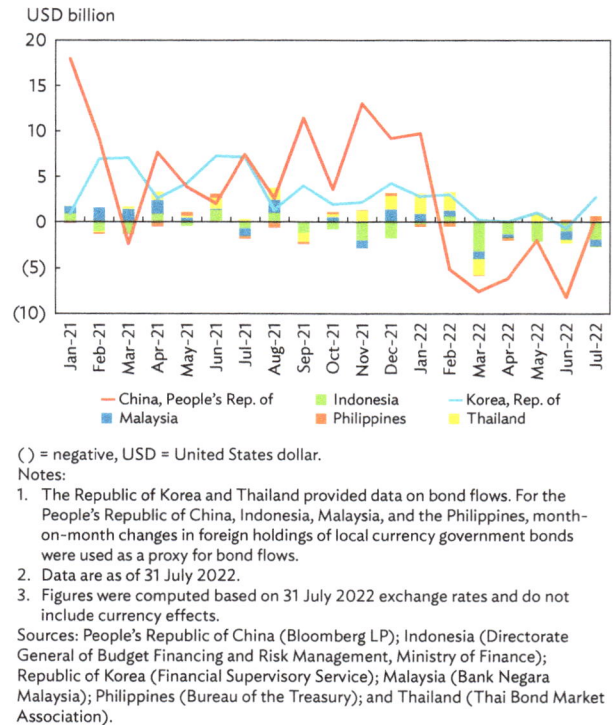

( ) = negative, USD = United States dollar.
Notes:
1. The Republic of Korea and Thailand provided data on bond flows. For the People's Republic of China, Indonesia, Malaysia, and the Philippines, month-on-month changes in foreign holdings of local currency government bonds were used as a proxy for bond flows.
2. Data are as of 31 July 2022.
3. Figures were computed based on 31 July 2022 exchange rates and do not include currency effects.
Sources: People's Republic of China (Bloomberg LP); Indonesia (Directorate General of Budget Financing and Risk Management, Ministry of Finance); Republic of Korea (Financial Supervisory Service); Malaysia (Bank Negara Malaysia); Philippines (Bureau of the Treasury); and Thailand (Thai Bond Market Association).

were recorded. After market sentiment improved in the second half of July, portfolio inflows were recorded in all regional markets except the Philippines (USD0.1 billion of outflows) between 1 August and 24 August, posting aggregate regional inflows of USD4.2 billion.

Tightened financial conditions led to capital outflows of USD21.5 billion from the region's bond markets during Q2 2022 (**Figure F**). As a result, foreign holdings declined in nearly all of the region's LCY bond markets during the quarter (**Figure G**). In Q2 2022, the Republic of Korea and Thailand were the only two bond markets that posted positive net inflows, particularly in May. In the Republic of Korea, sentiment was buoyed by news in the last week of April that it would seek inclusion in the FTSE's World Government Bond Index. In July, the Republic of Korea recorded capital inflows of USD2.7 billion on expectations of the removal of taxes on foreign bond purchases. In Thailand, market sentiment was boosted when the government announced that it would ease travel restrictions for foreigners on 1 June.

The risk outlook to the region remains tilted to the downside. In the short term, the region faces a moderation in the global and regional economic recoveries, and there are uncertainties regarding the containment of inflationary pressure, the pace of Federal Reserve tightening, the lingering impacts of the

Figure G: Foreign Holdings of Local Currency Government Bonds in Select Emerging East Asian Markets (% of total)

%

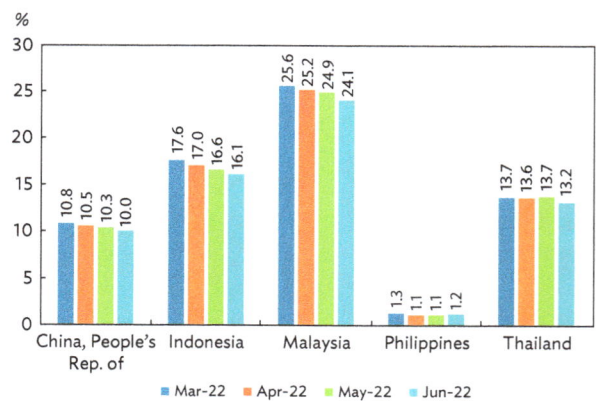

Sources: People's Republic of China (Bloomberg LP and CEIC Data Company); Indonesia (Directorate General of Budget Financing and Risk Management, Ministry of Finance); Malaysia (Bank Negara Malaysia); Philippines (Bureau of the Treasury); and Thailand (Bank of Thailand).

COVID-19 pandemic, possibly greater-than-expected negative spillover from the Russian invasion of Ukraine, and a bigger-than-expected slowdown in the PRC. As many major regional economies have committed to move to net-zero emissions, over the midterm the regional financial sector faces asset vulnerability issues, especially in high-emitting sectors, as well as large financing gaps for investments in both low-emission projects and the transitioning of high-emitting sectors. Providing enough financing for a resilient and timely transition, in a sustainable way, calls for policy support and will require continued market development and innovation in the financial sector.

Bond Market Developments in the Second Quarter of 2022

Size and Composition

Emerging East Asia's local currency bond market posted steady growth in the second quarter of 2022, reaching a size of USD22.9 trillion at the end of June.

The local currency (LCY) bond market in emerging East Asia expanded 3.1% quarter-on-quarter (q-o-q) in the second quarter (Q2) of 2022, the same pace of growth recorded in the preceding quarter, to reach a size of USD22.9 trillion at the end of June.[2] Growth in the government bond segment accelerated, as governments continued to issue sovereign debt to support economic recovery efforts amid heightened risks from global inflation, slowing global growth, and a more aggressive monetary policy stance by the United States (US) Federal Reserve. Expansion in the region's corporate bond market moderated due to maturities and reduced issuance caused by uncertainties and elevated borrowing costs, as several regional central banks tightened monetary policies to arrest rising inflation.

All nine LCY bond markets in emerging East Asia posted positive q-o-q growth in Q2 2022, although five of the nine markets expanded more slowly in Q2 2022 than in the first quarter (Q1) of 2022 (**Figure 1a**). Viet Nam experienced the fastest q-o-q growth, while the markets of Thailand and Indonesia showed the slowest q-o-q expansions in Q2 2022.

On a year-on-year basis (y-o-y), emerging East Asia's LCY bond market grew 14.0% in Q2 2022, up from 13.8% in the prior quarter. All nine markets recorded positive y-o-y growth rates during the review period, led by Viet Nam, Singapore, and the People's Republic of China (PRC) (**Figure 1b**). Six of the nine markets experienced weaker annual growth in Q2 2022 than in the previous quarter. The remaining markets of the PRC; Hong Kong, China; and Viet Nam experienced faster y-o-y expansions in Q2 2022 than in the prior quarter.

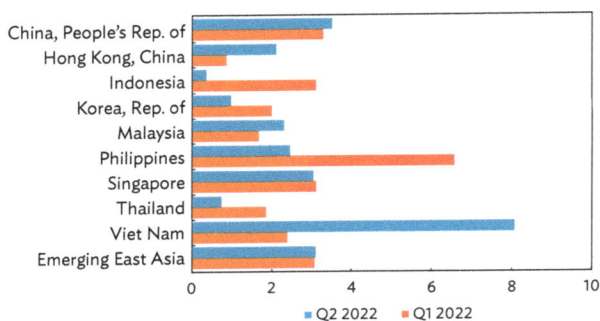

Figure 1a: Growth of Local Currency Bond Markets in the First and Second Quarters of 2022 (q-o-q, %)

q-o-q = quarter-on-quarter, Q1 = first quarter, Q2 = second quarter.
Notes:
1. For Singapore, corporate bonds outstanding are based on *AsianBondsOnline* estimates.
2. Growth rates are calculated from local currency base and do not include currency effects.
3. Emerging East Asia growth figures are based on 30 June 2022 currency exchange rates and do not include currency effects.
Sources: People's Republic of China (CEIC Data Company); Hong Kong, China (Hong Kong Monetary Authority); Indonesia (Bank Indonesia; Directorate General of Budget Financing and Risk Management, Ministry of Finance; and Indonesia Stock Exchange); Republic of Korea (KG Zeroin Corporation and The Bank of Korea); Malaysia (Bank Negara Malaysia); Philippines (Bureau of the Treasury and Bloomberg LP); Singapore (Monetary Authority of Singapore, Singapore Government Securities, and Bloomberg LP); Thailand (Bank of Thailand); and Viet Nam (Bloomberg LP and Vietnam Bond Market Association).

The PRC's LCY bond market continued to lead the region in size with an outstanding bond stock of USD18.4 trillion at the end of June. Its share of the region's total bond stock rose slightly to 80.2% at the end of Q2 2022 from 79.8% at the end of Q1 2022. Overall growth in the PRC's bond stock inched up to 3.5% q-o-q in Q2 2022 from 3.3% q-o-q in the prior quarter, supported by strong growth in the government bond segment. Growth in LCY government bonds outstanding rose to 4.3% q-o-q in Q2 2022 from 2.7% q-o-q in the previous quarter, driven primarily by a 7.5% q-o-q gain in local government bonds. The PRC's economic recovery stalled during the review period as authorities reinstated movement restrictions in key cities to quell the spread of fresh coronavirus disease (COVID-19) outbreaks. To revitalize the economy, local governments accelerated issuance of debt intended for infrastructure projects. Treasury bonds and policy bank bonds also supported the growth in government

---

[2] Emerging East Asia is defined to include Cambodia; the People's Republic of China; Hong Kong, China; Indonesia; the Republic of Korea; the Lao People's Democratic Republic; Malaysia; the Philippines; Singapore; Thailand; and Viet Nam.

Figure 1b: Growth of Local Currency Bond Markets in the First and Second Quarters of 2022 (y-o-y, %)

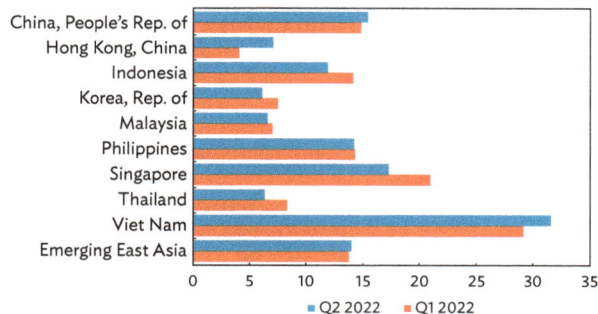

Q1 = first quarter, Q2 = second quarter, y-o-y = year-on-year.
Notes:
1. For Singapore, corporate bonds outstanding are based on *AsianBondsOnline* estimates.
2. Growth rates are calculated from local currency base and do not include currency effects.
3. Emerging East Asia growth figures are based on 30 June 2022 currency exchange rates and do not include currency effects.
Sources: People's Republic of China (CEIC Data Company); Hong Kong, China (Hong Kong Monetary Authority); Indonesia (Bank Indonesia; Directorate General of Budget Financing and Risk Management, Ministry of Finance; and Indonesia Stock Exchange); Republic of Korea (KG Zeroin Corporation and The Bank of Korea); Malaysia (Bank Negara Malaysia); Philippines (Bureau of the Treasury and Bloomberg LP); Singapore (Monetary Authority of Singapore, Singapore Government Securities, and Bloomberg LP); Thailand (Bank of Thailand); and Viet Nam (Bloomberg LP and Vietnam Bond Market Association).

bonds, rising 3.1% q-o-q and 0.5% q-o-q, respectively. Meanwhile, growth in the corporate bond segment eased to 2.0% q-o-q in Q2 2022 from 4.2% q-o-q in Q1 2022 amid "zero-COVID" restrictions and rising risks in the property sector. On a y-o-y basis, the PRC's LCY bond market expanded 15.4% in Q2 2022, up from 14.9% in the prior quarter.

The Republic of Korea remained the region's second-largest LCY bond market, with an outstanding bond stock of USD2.3 trillion at the end of June. The Republic of Korea's bond market accounted for 9.8% of the region's total LCY bonds outstanding at the end of June, down slightly from 10.0% at the end of March. Growth in the Republic of Korea's LCY bond market slowed to 1.0% q-o-q in Q2 2022 from 2.0% q-o-q in the previous quarter, as the expansion of both the government and corporate bond segments weakened. Government bonds outstanding rose 1.6% q-o-q in Q2 2022, down from 3.4% q-o-q in the previous quarter. Central government bonds continued to expand, rising 3.4% q-o-q in Q2 2022 after posting a 4.8% q-o-q gain in the previous quarter, as the government issued more debt to support economic recovery efforts. Other government

bonds rebounded in Q2 2022, rising 1.9% q-o-q after a contraction in the prior quarter. Meanwhile, central bank bonds declined 10.2% q-o-q in Q2 2022 following a 0.1% q-o-q drop in the previous quarter. Growth in corporate bonds outstanding eased to 0.5% q-o-q in Q2 2022 from 1.0% q-o-q in Q1 2022, as a relatively large volume of maturities outpaced a recovery in corporate debt issuance. On a y-o-y basis, growth in the Republic of Korea's LCY bond market moderated to 6.1% in Q2 2022 from 7.5% in the previous quarter.

Hong Kong, China's LCY bonds outstanding amounted to USD331.3 billion at the end of June. Overall growth rose to 2.1% q-o-q in Q2 2022 from 0.8% q-o-q in the previous quarter, driven primarily by a rebound in the corporate bond segment. The government bond segment posted marginal growth in Q2 2022 as Exchange Fund Bills (EFBs) outstanding recorded tepid growth of 0.2% q-o-q, while the stock of outstanding Exchange Fund Notes (EFNs) and Hong Kong Special Administrative Region bonds dropped 3.4% q-o-q and 0.4% q-o-q, respectively. Meanwhile, the outstanding stock of corporate bonds rose 4.4% q-o-q in Q2 2022, reversing the 1.9% q-o-q contraction in the prior quarter, due to increased issuance. Despite rising borrowing costs, corporate issuance jumped 15.6% q-o-q as business sentiment improved amid the easing of movement restrictions during the review period. On a y-o-y basis, growth in Hong Kong, China's LCY bond market moderated to 7.1% in Q2 2022 from 4.1% in the previous quarter.

The aggregate LCY bonds stock of the members of the Association of Southeast Asian Nations (ASEAN) rose 2.0% q-o-q and 11.8% y-o-y to reach USD1,962.7 billion at the end of June.[3] Growth eased from 2.8% q-o-q and 13.4% y-o-y in the previous quarter. ASEAN members' share of emerging Asia's total LCY bond market was little changed, slipping to 8.6% in Q2 2022 from 8.7% in the preceding quarter. The ASEAN LCY bond market comprised 73.2% government bonds (USD1,436.7 billion) and 26.8% corporate bonds (USD526.0 billion). The LCY bond markets of Singapore, Thailand, and Malaysia remained the largest in ASEAN, while Viet Nam accounted for the region's smallest market.

Singapore's LCY bond market reached a size of USD463.1 billion at the end of June. Overall growth slipped to 3.0% q-o-q in Q2 2022 from 3.1% in Q1 2022.

---

[3] LCY bond statistics for ASEAN include the markets of Indonesia, Malaysia, the Philippines, Singapore, Thailand, and Viet Nam.

The outstanding stock of LCY government bonds rose 3.8% q-o-q during the review period, supported by growth in Monetary Authority of Singapore (MAS) bills (5.7% q-o-q) and Singapore Government Securities (2.0% q-o-q). The corporate bond segment expanded 1.4% q-o-q in Q2 2022 after a marginal contraction in the previous quarter, driven by a recovery in issuance. Corporate debt issuance jumped 113.0% q-o-q on improved business sentiment as almost all domestic and border restrictions were progressively removed during the review period. On an annual basis, Singapore's LCY bond market expanded 17.3% y-o-y in Q2 2022, down from 20.9% y-o-y in the previous quarter.

The outstanding stock of LCY bonds in Thailand amounted to USD427.3 billion at the end of June. Quarterly growth dropped to 0.7% in Q2 2022 from 1.8% in Q1 2022 due largely to a contraction in the government bond segment. Outstanding LCY government bonds declined 0.7% q-o-q in Q2 2022, reversing the 2.1% q-o-q growth in the previous quarter. The decline in government bonds stemmed from a contraction in Bank of Thailand (BOT) bonds (–8.9% q-o-q), which outpaced growth in government bonds and Treasury bills (2.3% q-o-q), and in state-owned enterprise and other bonds (1.0% q-o-q). Meanwhile, growth in the corporate bond segment jumped to 4.6% q-o-q in Q2 2022 from 1.2% q-o-q in the previous quarter on the back of strong issuance. Issuance of corporate bonds rose 36.3% q-o-q in Q2 2022 as corporates continued to issue debt while borrowing costs remained low. The BOT was among the last regional banks to engage in monetary policy tightening and had kept its policy rate at a record low of 0.50% during the review period before raising it by 25 basis points (bps) in August. On an annual basis, Thailand's LCY bond market posted 6.4% y-o-y growth in Q2 2022, down from 8.4% y-o-y in Q1 2022.

Malaysia's outstanding LCY bond stock totaled USD409.5 billion at the end of June. Overall growth rose to 2.3% q-o-q in Q2 2022 from 1.7% q-o-q in the prior quarter, driven primarily by growth in the government bond segment. Government bonds outstanding rose 4.1% q-o-q in Q2 2021, up from 2.8% q-o-q in the previous quarter. Central government bonds drove much of the growth. Although Bank Negara Malaysia (BNM) resumed bond issuance during the review period, the share of central bank bonds to total government bonds remained minimal. Growth in Malaysia's corporate bond market weakened further to 0.1% q-o-q in Q2 2022 from

0.3% q-o-q in the previous quarter due to a relatively high volume of maturities, which outstripped a rebound in issuance. Borrowing costs also rose, as BNM increased its overnight policy rate by 25 bps in May. On a y-o-y basis, Malaysia's LCY bond market expanded 6.6% in Q2 2022, down from 7.0% q-o-q in the previous quarter.

Malaysia remained home to the largest *sukuk* (Islamic bond) market in emerging East Asia. At the end of June, Malaysia's *sukuk* market reached a size of USD258.4 billion on growth of 1.5% q-o-q. Government *sukuk* outstanding amounted to USD110.8 billion, representing 48.1% of Malaysia's total LCY government bond stock. The corporate bond market remained dominated by *sukuk*: outstanding corporate *sukuk* totaled USD147.6 billion, accounting for 82.4% of the total LCY corporate bond stock.

Outstanding LCY bonds in Indonesia rose 0.3% q-o-q and 11.9 % y-o-y in Q2 2022 to reach USD369.0 billion at the end of June. Overall growth dropped from 3.1% q-o-q and 14.1% y-o-y in Q1 2022 due to weak growth in the government bond segment and a contraction in the corporate bond segment. Government bonds outstanding posted a 0.6% q-o-q gain in Q2 2022, down from a 3.0% q-o-q rise in the previous quarter. A contraction in central bank bonds (–2.0% q-o-q) outpaced the growth in central government bonds (0.4% q-o-q) and nontradable bonds (8.0% q-o-q) during the review period. The corporate bond market contracted 2.3% q-o-q in Q2 2022 due mainly to a decline in issuance amid uncertainties in the growth outlook.

Indonesia's *sukuk* market expanded 4.4% in Q2 2022, reaching a size of USD67.3 billion at the end of June. *Sukuk* outstanding comprised 18.2% of Indonesia's LCY bond market. Government *sukuk* outstanding totaled USD64.8 billion, accounting for 19.1% of Indonesia's LCY government bond market. Outstanding corporate *sukuk* stood at USD2.5 billion, or 8.5% of Indonesia's LCY corporate bond market.

In the Philippines, the outstanding stock of LCY bonds totaled USD194.3 billion at the end of June. Overall growth moderated to 2.4% q-o-q in Q2 2022 from 6.5% q-o-q in the previous quarter due largely to a contraction in the corporate bond segment. Government bonds outstanding rose 4.1% q-o-q in Q2 2022, supported by robust growth in Bangko Sentral ng Pilipinas securities (38.3% q-o-q) and other government bonds (28.8% q-o-q). Growth in Treasury bonds also contributed to the expansion. On the other hand, Treasury bills posted a 17.1% q-o-q decline during the review period. Corporate bonds outstanding contracted 7.1% q-o-q in Q2 2022 as rising interest rates curtailed debt issuance. The Bangko Sentral ng Pilipinas raised its benchmark rate by 25 bps each in May and June. On a y-o-y basis, the expansion in the Philippines' LCY bond market inched down to 14.2% in Q2 2022 from 14.3% in the previous quarter.

With USD99.5 billion of outstanding bonds at the end of June, Viet Nam's LCY bond market remained the smallest in emerging East Asia. Starting from a relatively small base, Viet Nam's bond market posted the highest quarterly (8.1% q-o-q) and annual (31.6% y-o-y) growth rates in the region during the review period. Quarterly growth more than doubled from 2.4% q-o-q in the previous quarter as growth in both the government and corporate bond segments accelerated. Growth in government bonds outstanding soared to 7.4% q-o-q in Q2 2022 from 1.5% q-o-q in the previous quarter due primarily to robust growth in central bank bills and a rebound in government-guaranteed and municipal bonds. Growth in the corporate bond segment jumped to 9.5% q-o-q in Q2 2022 from 4.6% q-o-q in the prior quarter, driven by a rebound in issuance as borrowing costs remained relatively low. The State Bank of Vietnam is the sole central bank in the region that has yet to pivot from the dovish policy stance adopted during the pandemic.

Government bonds continued to dominate emerging East Asia's LCY bond market. The region's outstanding government bonds reached USD14.5 trillion at the end of June, comprising 63.1% of the region's total LCY bond market (**Table 1**). Growth in the region's government bonds quickened to 3.9% q-o-q in Q2 2022 from 2.8% q-o-q in Q1 2022. Except for Thailand, all of the region's LCY government bond markets saw positive q-o-q growth in Q2 2022, supported by strong issuance in nearly all markets. Most of the region's governments continued to issue debt to safeguard economic recovery amid heightened uncertainties from global inflation and the Federal Reserve's accelerated pace of policy normalization. The PRC, for instance, stepped up issuance of local government bonds to fund infrastructure projects to revitalize its slowing economy. Annual growth in the region's government bond market increased to 15.5% y-o-y in Q2 2022 from 14.8% y-o-y in the prior quarter.

The PRC's government bond market remained the largest in the region, followed by the Republic of Korea's. Together, the two markets accounted for 88.9% of the region's total LCY government bond stock at the end of June. ASEAN member economies accounted for 9.9% of the region's government bond market. Within ASEAN, the largest government bond markets were those of Indonesia and Singapore, while the smallest was that of Viet Nam.

Emerging East Asia's LCY government bonds remained concentrated in medium- to long-term tenors at the end of June (**Figure 2**). About 55.2% of the region's total government bonds had maturities of longer than 5 years. Apart from Hong Kong, China and the Philippines, all markets in the region had over half of their government bonds concentrated in tenors of 5 years or longer. As in the previous quarter, Hong Kong, China's government bond segment remained dominated by shorter-term bonds due to strong market demand for shorter-dated securities. The Philippines' bond market saw a slight shift in its maturity profile: the share of bonds with maturities of 5 years or longer dropped to 43.1% in Q2 2022 from 50.3% in the prior quarter.

Emerging East Asia's corporate bond market reached a size of USD8.4 trillion at the end of June, representing 36.9% of the region's total LCY bond stock. Growth eased to 1.7% q-o-q and 11.5% y-o-y in Q2 2022 from 3.4% q-o-q and 12.1% y-o-y in the previous quarter. Except for the markets of Indonesia and the Philippines, all of the region's corporate bond markets showed positive q-o-q growth in Q2 2022. Those that posted positive q-o-q growth, however, mostly experienced a slowdown in growth as higher interest rates curtailed corporate borrowing. Borrowing costs in the region generally rose during the review period as several central banks tightened their monetary policies to combat inflation.

The corporate bond markets of the PRC and the Republic of Korea remained the largest in emerging East Asia, accounting for 76.6% and 15.3%, respectively, of the region's total corporate bonds outstanding at the end of June. Meanwhile, the combined shares of ASEAN member economies added up to 6.2% of the region's total corporate bond stock. Within ASEAN, Malaysia remained home to the largest LCY corporate bond market, followed by Singapore and Thailand.

Table 1: Size and Composition of Local Currency Bond Markets

	Q2 2021		Q1 2022		Q2 2022		Growth Rate (LCY-base %)				Growth Rate (USD-base %)			
							Q2 2021		Q2 2022		Q2 2021		Q2 2022	
	Amount (USD billion)	% share	Amount (USD billion)	% share	Amount (USD billion)	% share	q-o-q	y-o-y	q-o-q	y-o-y	q-o-q	y-o-y	q-o-q	y-o-y
China, People's Rep. of														
Total	16,507	100.0	18,755	100.0	18,368	100.0	3.0	14.4	3.5	15.4	4.5	25.1	(2.1)	11.3
Government	10,591	64.2	12,051	64.3	11,898	64.8	3.3	16.2	4.3	16.6	4.8	27.1	(1.3)	12.3
Corporate	5,917	35.8	6,704	35.7	6,469	35.2	2.3	11.3	2.0	13.4	3.9	21.8	(3.5)	9.3
Hong Kong, China														
Total	313	100.0	325	100.0	331	100.0	(0.8)	7.0	2.1	7.1	(0.7)	6.8	1.9	6.0
Government	157	50.1	174	53.4	173	52.4	2.4	5.1	0.04	12.0	2.5	4.9	(0.1)	10.8
Corporate	156	49.9	151	46.6	158	47.6	(3.7)	8.9	4.4	2.2	(3.6)	8.7	4.3	1.2
Indonesia														
Total	339	100.0	381	100.0	369	100.0	2.4	30.6	0.3	11.9	2.5	28.5	(3.2)	8.9
Government	310	91.4	350	91.8	339	92.0	2.8	34.8	0.6	12.7	3.0	32.6	(3.0)	9.6
Corporate	29	8.6	31	8.2	29	8.0	(2.4)	(1.6)	(2.3)	4.0	(2.2)	(3.2)	(5.7)	1.2
Korea, Rep. of														
Total	2,448	100.0	2,391	100.0	2,253	100.0	2.3	7.9	1.0	6.1	2.8	15.3	(5.8)	(8.0)
Government	1,029	42.0	1,009	42.2	956	42.4	3.2	11.6	1.6	7.2	3.7	19.2	(5.2)	(7.0)
Corporate	1,419	58.0	1,383	57.8	1,296	57.6	1.6	5.4	0.5	5.4	2.1	12.6	(6.2)	(8.6)
Malaysia														
Total	408	100.0	420	100.0	410	100.0	2.7	8.9	2.3	6.6	2.6	12.5	(2.5)	0.3
Government	223	54.6	232	55.3	230	56.3	3.9	11.5	4.1	9.9	3.8	15.2	(0.8)	3.4
Corporate	185	45.4	188	44.7	179	43.7	1.3	6.0	0.1	2.6	1.2	9.5	(4.6)	(3.4)
Philippines														
Total	192	100.0	201	100.0	194	100.0	2.5	25.1	2.4	14.2	1.9	27.6	(3.6)	1.4
Government	160	83.8	172	85.5	169	86.8	3.9	32.7	4.1	18.4	3.3	35.4	(2.0)	5.1
Corporate	31	16.2	29	14.5	26	13.2	(3.9)	(3.6)	(7.1)	(7.2)	(4.5)	(1.6)	(12.6)	(17.6)
Singapore														
Total	408	100.0	461	100.0	463	100.0	6.2	16.3	3.0	17.3	6.2	20.4	0.4	13.5
Government	272	66.6	318	68.8	321	69.3	4.8	19.7	3.8	22.0	4.7	24.0	1.1	18.0
Corporate	136	33.4	144	31.2	142	30.7	9.3	10.0	1.4	7.9	9.2	13.9	(1.3)	4.4
Thailand														
Total	443	100.0	451	100.0	427	100.0	2.6	5.6	0.7	6.4	44.7	59.5	(5.2)	(3.6)
Government	322	72.7	329	72.9	307	71.9	1.7	6.1	(0.7)	5.2	42.5	54.8	(6.6)	(4.6)
Corporate	121	27.3	122	27.1	120	28.1	5.1	4.4	4.6	9.5	50.9	73.3	(1.6)	(0.8)
Viet Nam														
Total	76	100.0	94	100.0	99	100.0	6.1	27.6	8.1	31.6	6.3	28.6	6.0	30.0
Government	59	77.1	66	70.6	70	70.2	(0.5)	14.7	7.4	19.8	(0.2)	15.6	5.4	18.4
Corporate	17	22.9	28	29.4	30	29.8	36.4	105.1	9.5	71.4	36.8	106.7	7.5	69.4
Emerging East Asia														
Total	21,134	100.0	23,480	100.0	22,914	100.0	2.9	13.6	3.1	14.0	4.8	23.9	(2.4)	8.4
Government	13,121	62.1	14,700	62.6	14,465	63.1	3.3	16.0	3.9	15.5	5.3	26.5	(1.6)	10.2
Corporate	8,012	37.9	8,780	37.4	8,450	36.9	2.2	10.0	1.7	11.5	3.9	19.8	(3.8)	5.5
Japan														
Total	11,520	100.0	10,843	100.0	9,659	100.0	(0.4)	7.0	(0.7)	2.4	(0.7)	4.0	(10.9)	(16.2)
Government	10,691	92.8	10,067	92.8	8,957	92.7	(0.6)	7.0	(0.8)	2.3	(0.9)	3.9	(11.0)	(16.2)
Corporate	829	7.2	776	7.2	702	7.3	2.6	7.5	0.9	3.4	2.3	4.4	(9.5)	(15.3)

( ) = negative, LCY = local currency, q-o-q = quarter-on-quarter, Q1 = first quarter, Q2 = second quarter, USD = United States dollar, y-o-y = year-on-year.

Notes:
1. For Singapore, corporate bonds outstanding are based on *AsianBondsOnline* estimates.
2. Corporate bonds include issues by financial institutions.
3. Bloomberg LP end-of-period LCY–USD rates are used.
4. For LCY base, emerging East Asia growth figures based on 30 June 2022 currency exchange rates and do not include currency effects.
5. Emerging East Asia is defined to include Cambodia; the People's Republic of China; Hong Kong, China; Indonesia; the Republic of Korea; the Lao People's Democratic Republic; Malaysia; the Philippines; Singapore; Thailand; and Viet Nam.

Sources: People's Republic of China (CEIC Data Company); Hong Kong, China (Hong Kong Monetary Authority); Indonesia (Bank Indonesia; Directorate General of Budget Financing and Risk Management, Ministry of Finance; and Indonesia Stock Exchange); Republic of Korea (KG Zeroin Corporation and The Bank of Korea); Malaysia (Bank Negara Malaysia); Philippines (Bureau of the Treasury and Bloomberg LP); Singapore (Monetary Authority of Singapore, Singapore Government Securities, and Bloomberg LP); Thailand (Bank of Thailand); Viet Nam (Bloomberg LP and Vietnam Bond Market Association); and Japan (Japan Securities Dealers Association).

Figure 2: Maturity Structure of Local Currency Government Bonds Outstanding in Emerging East Asia

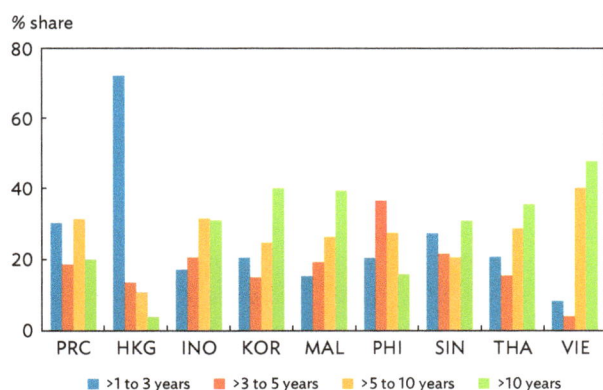

PRC = China, People's Rep. of; HKG = Hong Kong, China; INO = Indonesia; KOR = Korea, Rep. of; MAL = Malaysia; PHI = Philippines; SIN = Singapore; THA = Thailand; VIE = Viet Nam.
Notes:
1. Government bonds include Treasury bills and bonds.
2. Data as of 30 June 2022.
Source: *AsianBondsOnline*.

Table 2: Size and Composition of Local Currency Bond Markets (% of GDP)

	Q2 2021	Q1 2022	Q2 2022
China, People's Rep. of			
Total	97.8	102.0	104.6
Government	62.8	65.5	67.7
Corporate	35.1	36.5	36.8
Hong Kong, China			
Total	87.4	89.4	91.3
Government	43.8	47.8	47.8
Corporate	43.6	41.6	43.5
Indonesia			
Total	30.8	31.3	30.1
Government	28.1	28.7	27.7
Corporate	2.6	2.6	2.4
Korea, Rep. of			
Total	146.8	150.2	150.6
Government	61.7	63.4	63.9
Corporate	85.1	86.9	86.6
Malaysia			
Total	121.9	125.7	125.9
Government	66.5	69.5	70.8
Corporate	55.4	56.2	55.1
Philippines			
Total	50.5	52.2	51.9
Government	42.3	44.6	45.0
Corporate	8.2	7.6	6.8
Singapore			
Total	108.8	114.3	114.8
Government	72.5	78.7	79.6
Corporate	36.3	35.6	35.2
Thailand			
Total	89.2	91.3	90.2
Government	64.8	66.6	64.8
Corporate	24.4	24.7	25.4
Viet Nam			
Total	22.8	25.0	26.2
Government	17.6	17.7	18.4
Corporate	5.2	7.3	7.8
Emerging East Asia			
Total	96.4	99.7	101.4
Government	59.9	62.4	64.0
Corporate	36.6	37.3	37.4
Japan			
Total	236.0	243.7	241.3
Government	219.0	226.2	223.8
Corporate	17.0	17.4	17.5

GDP = gross domestic product, Q1 = first quarter, Q2 = second quarter.
Notes:
1. Data for GDP is from CEIC Data Company.
2. For Singapore, corporate bonds outstanding are based on *AsianBondsOnline* estimates.
Sources: People's Republic of China (CEIC Data Company); Hong Kong, China (Hong Kong Monetary Authority); Indonesia (Bank Indonesia; Directorate General of Budget Financing and Risk Management, Ministry of Finance; and Indonesia Stock Exchange); Republic of Korea (KG Zeroin Corporation and The Bank of Korea); Malaysia (Bank Negara Malaysia); Philippines (Bureau of the Treasury and Bloomberg LP); Singapore (Monetary Authority of Singapore, Singapore Government Securities, and Bloomberg LP); Thailand (Bank of Thailand); Viet Nam (Bloomberg LP and Vietnam Bond Market Association); and Japan (Japan Securities Dealers Association).

At the end of Q2 2022, outstanding LCY bonds in emerging East Asia were equivalent to 101.4% of the total gross domestic product (GDP) of the region, up from the 99.7% share recorded in the previous quarter (**Table 2**). The increased share was supported by government bonds, which accounted for the equivalent of 64.0% of regional GDP during the review period, up from 62.4% in the prior quarter. The bonds-to-GDP share of corporate bonds in Q2 2022, on the other hand, was up from 37.3% in Q1 2022 to 37.4% in Q2 2022. Some economies accelerated their fundraising activities due to expectations of higher borrowing costs in the coming months as the Federal Reserve and other regional markets hiked interest rates in an effort to combat high inflation. Corporate bond market growth, however, was curtailed by uncertainties caused by high inflation and risks to the global economy.

Four economies in emerging East Asia had an LCY bonds-to-GDP share above 100% at the end of the review period. The Republic of Korea led the region at 150.6%, followed by Malaysia (125.9%), Singapore (114.8%), and the PRC (104.6%). Viet Nam continued to trail all economies in the region, having a bonds-to-GDP share of only 26.2%.

An increase in the size of the LCY bond market as a percentage of GDP from Q1 2022 to Q2 2022 was observed in the PRC; Hong Kong, China;

the Republic of Korea; Malaysia; Singapore; and Viet Nam. The following economies showed an increase in their respective government bonds-to-GDP shares: the PRC, the Republic of Korea, Malaysia, the Philippines, Singapore, and Viet Nam; while Hong Kong, China's government bonds-to-GDP share was barely changed. On the other hand, for corporate bonds, only the PRC; Hong Kong, China; Thailand; and Viet Nam posted an increase from Q1 2022 to Q2 2022.

During the review period, Singapore had the largest government bonds-to-GDP share in emerging East Asia (79.6%), while the smallest was recorded in Viet Nam (18.4%). For LCY corporate bonds, the economy with the highest share of corporate bonds to GDP was the Republic of Korea (86.6%), while Indonesia had the smallest (2.4%).

Foreign Investor Holdings and Foreign Bond Flows

A foreign sell-off in the region led to a decline in foreign holdings of emerging East Asian bonds in Q2 2022.

Foreign holdings in emerging East Asian bond markets continued to decline in Q2 2022 (**Figure 3**). The aggressive monetary policy tightening of the

Federal Reserve to address high inflation led to a surge in US Treasury yields and the strengthening of the US dollar, resulting in a sell-off in the region's bond markets. Moreover, expectations of further monetary tightening in the US and by other central banks in the region amid persistent high inflation, volatility in global yields, and concerns of a global economic slowdown continued to make emerging East Asia's bond returns less attractive.

The region registered a record USD21.5 billion of net foreign outflows from the bond market in Q2 2022, the first since USD4.0 billion of net outflows occurred in Q1 2020 at the start of the pandemic and a reversal from the USD2.2 billion of net inflows posted in Q1 2022 (**Figure 4**). Foreign investors sold a net USD8.1 billion and USD2.3 billion of emerging East Asian LCY bonds in the months of April and May, respectively. June saw the biggest sell-off at USD11.1 billion as nearly all markets, except for the Philippines, recorded net outflows following the 75 bps rate hike by the Federal Reserve on 15 June.

The PRC led the sell-off in the region, posting net outflows of USD6.2 billion, USD2.1 billion, and USD8.3 billion in the months of April, May, and

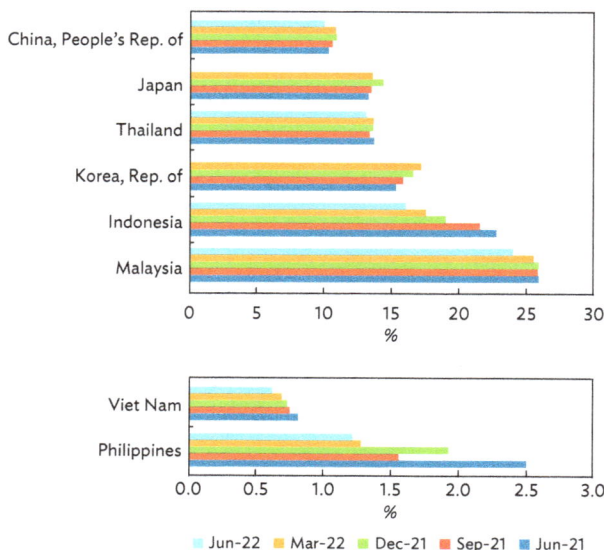

Figure 3: Foreign Holdings of Local Currency Government Bonds in Select Asian Markets (% of total)

Note: Data for Japan and the Republic of Korea are as of 31 March 2022.
Source: *AsianBondsOnline* calculations based on data from local market sources.

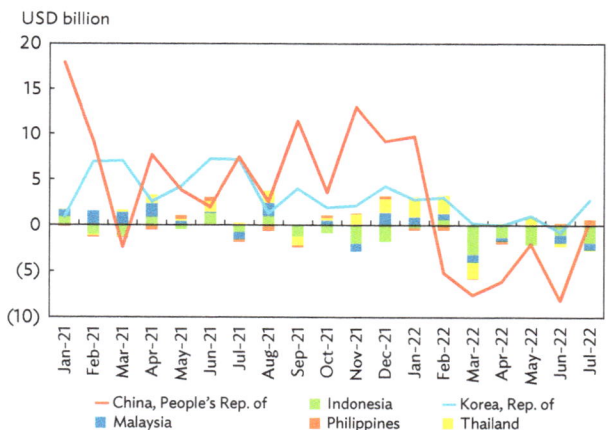

Figure 4: Foreign Capital Flows in Local Currency Bond Markets in Emerging East Asia

( ) = negative, USD = United States dollar.
Notes:
1. The Republic of Korea and Thailand provided data on bond flows. For the People's Republic of China, Indonesia, Malaysia, and the Philippines, month-on-month changes in foreign holdings of local currency government bonds were used as a proxy for bond flows.
2. Data are as of 31 July 2022.
3. Figures were computed based on 31 July 2022 exchange rates and do not include currency effects.
Sources: People's Republic of China (Bloomberg LP); Indonesia (Directorate General of Budget Financing and Risk Management, Ministry of Finance); Republic of Korea (Financial Supervisory Service); Malaysia (Bank Negara Malaysia); Philippines (Bureau of the Treasury); and Thailand (Thai Bond Market Association).

June, respectively. June marked the fifth consecutive month of net outflows from the PRC bond market. Net outflows totaled USD16.6 billion in Q2 2022, up from USD3.2 billion in the previous quarter. Diverging monetary policies between the People's Bank of China (PBOC) and the Federal Reserve led to a further drop in foreign holdings in the PRC's bond market to 10.0% in Q2 2022 from 10.8% in Q1 2022. The PRC's domestic bonds used to offer higher premiums but the recent aggressive hikes by the Federal Reserve, with the PBOC maintaining an accommodative stance, has led to weakening foreign demand. Risks of an economic slowdown, exacerbated by the resumption of community lockdowns, also contributed to capital outflows from the domestic bond market. In July, the PRC's domestic bond market registered net inflows of USD0.5 billion; however, this was very low compared to inflows from last year.

The global sell-off following the Federal Reserve's rate hike in June drove the decline in foreign holdings in the rest of the region's markets. Malaysia continued to have the highest foreign holdings share in the region at 24.1% at the end of June, but it also registered the largest quarterly decline (1.5 percentage points) in the foreign holdings share. This was brought about by USD1.2 billion of net outflows in Q2 2022, reversing the USD0.8 billion of net inflows posted in Q1 2022. Malaysia posted net foreign inflows in May of USD0.1 billion; however, this was offset by the net outflows of USD0.4 billion and USD0.9 billion in April and June, respectively. In July, Malaysia continued to register net outflows of USD0.8 billion.

In Indonesia, the foreign holdings share fell to 16.1% from 17.6% during the same period. The relatively accommodative stance of Bank Indonesia compared to other central banks in the region may have also contributed to the decline in foreign demand for domestic bonds as Indonesia used to offer higher returns. Indonesia registered the second-largest net outflows in the region in Q2 2022 at USD4.6 billion, up from USD2.9 billion in the previous quarter, with net outflows recorded in each month of the quarter. Foreign investors sold domestic bonds worth USD1.4 billion, USD2.2 billion, and USD1.0 billion, respectively, in April, May, and June. In July, net foreign outflows rose to USD2.0 billion.

In Thailand, the foreign holdings share fell to 13.2% in Q2 2022 from 13.7% in Q1 2022. The marginal change was due to the bond market posting net inflows of USD0.6 billion during the quarter, down from the USD2.3 billion posted in Q1 2022. However, Thailand was not spared during the regional sell-off in June as it registered USD0.4 billion of net outflows. This was offset by the net inflows of USD0.2 billion and USD0.8 billion in April and May, respectively. In July, Thailand posted net foreign outflows of USD0.1 billion.

In the Philippines, the foreign holdings share remained negligible at 1.2%, a slight decline from 1.3% in the previous quarter. The Philippines registered net inflows in May and June of USD0.03 billion and USD0.24 billion, respectively. However, these were offset by the USD0.31 billion of outflows in April that resulted in net quarterly outflows of USD0.05 billion in Q2 2022. In July, the Philippines recorded net foreign inflows of USD0.6 billion. In Viet Nam, the foreign holdings share remained negligible at 0.6% in Q2 2022, inching down from 0.7% in Q1 2022.

In the Republic of Korea, the foreign holdings share rose to 17.2% at the end of Q1 2022, the latest quarter for which data are available, from 16.6% at the end of December 2021. The Republic of Korea remained a safe haven for foreign investors during the start of the year, and it maintained a relatively higher interest rate differential with US Treasuries as the Bank of Korea also proceeded with rate hikes in 2022. However, in Q2 2022, foreign demand weakened as US Treasury yields rose at a faster pace, resulting in a decline in the risk premiums offered by domestic bonds. The Republic of Korea's LCY bond market registered small inflows of USD0.03 billion and USD1.05 billion in April and May, respectively. In June, it incurred outflows of USD0.7 billion, the first monthly outflows since December 2020. Increased expectations of an economic slowdown brought about by an acceleration in inflation and weaker export growth also contributed to muted foreign demand for domestic bonds. In July, however, foreign investors returned to the market with net inflows of USD2.7 billion, following the Federal Reserve's dovish comments at its July meeting, leading investors to anticipate a slowdown in its monetary policy tightening.

Domestic investors continued to play an important role in the region's LCY government bond markets. With the decline in foreign holdings, government bond markets in the region saw increased participation from domestic investors, particularly banks and insurance companies and pension funds (**Figure 5**). Central banks also were active investors in the government bond market, providing stability and supporting regional governments' fiscal measures.

Figure 5: Investor Profiles of Local Currency Government Bonds in Select Emerging East Asian Markets

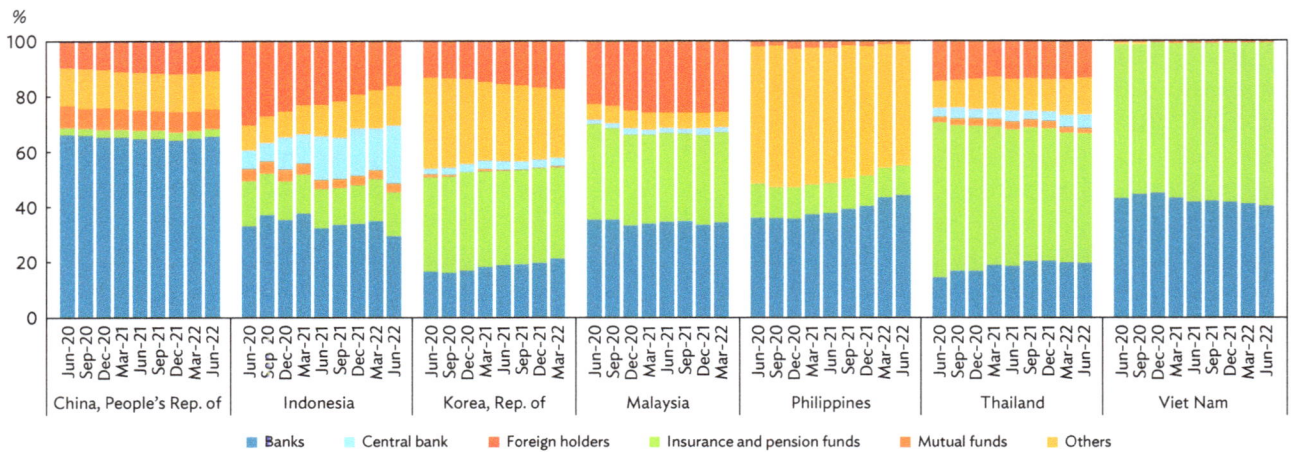

Notes:
1. Data for the Republic of Korea and Malaysia are up to March 2022.
2. "Others" include government institutions, individuals, securities companies, custodians, private corporations, and all other investors not elsewhere classified.
Source: AsianBondsOnline.

Local Currency Bond Issuance

Local currency bond issuance in emerging East Asia totaled USD2.4 trillion in the second quarter of 2022, buoyed by higher sales in nearly all markets.

Emerging East Asia's LCY bond sales rebounded in Q2 2022 with record-high quarterly issuance of USD2.4 trillion (**Figure 6**). All regional markets except Indonesia posted increased issuance during the quarter.

The PRC was the largest contributor to the surge in regional issuance, with its share of the regional total expanding from 66.5% in Q1 2022 to 68.1% in Q2 2022. On the other hand, the respective shares of the Republic of Korea (from 8.5% in Q1 2022 to 7.9% in Q2 2022) and Hong Kong, China (from 7.0% in Q1 2022 to 6.4% in Q2 2022) contracted by 0.6 percentage points each. The combined share of ASEAN markets shed 0.5 percentage points during the quarter to 17.5% from 18.0% in Q1 2022.

Government bonds accounted for the bulk of the new bonds issued during the quarter as their share of the regional total swelled to 47.8% in Q2 2022 from 40.1% in the previous quarter (**Figure 7**). Issuance by governments picked up during the quarter as part of frontloading strategies in place in the first half of the year to bolster fragile economic recoveries in most emerging East Asian

markets amid weakening global financial conditions and ahead of rising interest rates in the US and the region. Corporate bonds' share of total regional issuance continued to decline in Q2 2022, falling to 34.0% from 40.5% in Q1 2022, over uncertainties in the economic outlook. Central bank issuance saw its share of the regional issuance total slipping to 18.2% in Q2 2022.

Figure 6: Local Currency Bond Issuance in Emerging East Asia

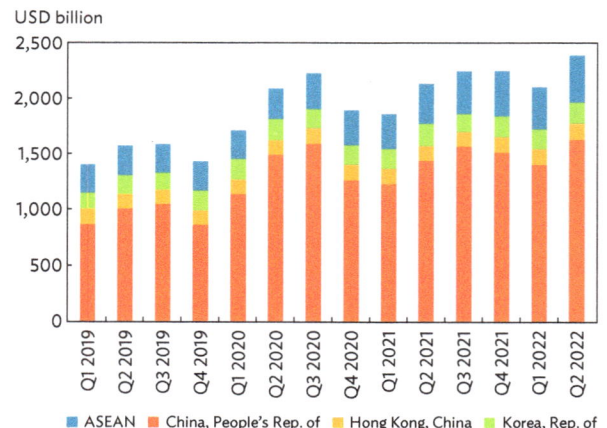

ASEAN = Association of Southeast Asian Nations, Q1 = first quarter, Q2 = second quarter, Q3 = third quarter, Q4 = fourth quarter, USD = United States dollar.
Notes:
1. ASEAN includes the markets of Indonesia, Malaysia, the Philippines, Singapore, Thailand, and Viet Nam.
2. Figures were computed based on 30 June 2022 currency exchange rates and do not include currency effects.
Source: AsianBondsOnline.

Figure 7: Issuance Volume by Type of Bonds

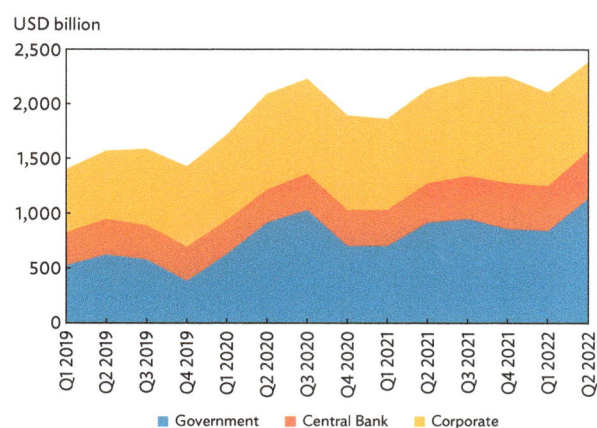

USD billion

Q1 = first quarter, Q2 = second quarter, Q3 = third quarter, Q4 = fourth quarter, USD = United States dollar.
Note: Figures were computed based on 30 June 2022 currency exchange rates and do not include currency effects.
Source: *AsianBondsOnline*.

government bonds issued with maturities of 5 years or less accounted for 50.5% of the regional issuance total during the quarter, while those with maturities of more than 5 years had a share of 49.5% (**Figure 8**). Notably, the share of longer-tenor bonds significantly declined from 56.6% in Q1 2022, indicating investors' risk preference for short-dated instruments amid weakening global financial conditions. In particular, the share of bonds with tenors from more than 1 year to 3 years climbed to 33.4% in Q2 2022 from 25.9% in the earlier quarter.

On a q-o-q basis, LCY bond issuance in emerging East Asia rebounded on growth of 13.4% in Q2 2022 from a 6.5% contraction in Q1 2022. Almost all emerging East Asian markets saw increased issuance of bonds in Q2 2022 versus Q1 2022, with Indonesia as the sole exception as it reduced issuance across all bond types (**Table 3**).

The government bond segment was the main driver of growth in Q2 2022 as issuance of corporate bonds continued to decline. Overall growth in government bond issuance rebounded to 25.9% q-o-q in Q2 2022 after falling 2.3% q-o-q in the prior quarter.

Treasury and other government bonds comprised the fastest-growing bond segment in terms of issuance, with their growth rising 35.3% q-o-q in Q2 2022 following a contraction of 2.3% q-o-q in Q1 2022. Some governments continued to issue bonds as part of a frontloading strategy to support fiscal spending in the first half of the year. Issuance of Treasury and other government bonds tallied USD1,143.6 billion in Q2 2022 and accounted for 72.5% of the aggregate government bond issuance. All emerging East Asian markets recorded q-o-q increases in the issuance of Treasury and other government bonds except for Indonesia, the Philippines, and Viet Nam.

In Q2 2022, the maturity structure of the region's LCY government bond issuances was broadly balanced between short-term and long-term tenors. New

Amid rising inflation, the region's central banks saw issuance growth of 6.5% q-o-q in Q2 2022, reversing the decline of 2.3% q-o-q in Q1 2022. Total issuance reached USD434.5 billion, representing 27.5% of aggregate government bond issuance in Q2 2022. However, growth in central bank issuance was capped as only five central banks in the region recorded higher issuance volumes during the quarter. The Hong Kong Monetary Authority, Bangko Sentral ng Pilipinas, Monetary Authority of Singapore, and State Bank of Vietnam all increased their issuance of central bank instruments, while BNM resumed issuance of central bank bills.

In Q2 2022, corporate bond issuance contracted 4.9% q-o-q, albeit at a slower pace than the 12.0% q-o-q decline in Q1 2022. Six out of the nine markets in emerging East Asia posted increased issuance of corporate bonds during the quarter. Overall growth of the corporate bond segment, however, was dragged down by a slowdown in issuance in the PRC and, to a lesser extent, in Indonesia and the Philippines.

On a y-o-y basis, growth in LCY bond issuance in emerging East Asia moderated to 11.8% in Q2 2022 from 13.0% in Q1 2022. Similar with the q-o-q trends, the government bond segment led the region's growth amid a tapering of issuance by corporates. The bond markets of Indonesia, the Republic of Korea, and Thailand all recorded y-o-y contractions in issuance volume in Q2 2022.

LCY bond issuance in the PRC rebounded strongly in Q2 2022, posting growth of 16.3% q-o-q after declining 7.6% q-o-q in Q1 2022. Total issuance reached USD1,629.2 billion in Q2 2022, with the government bond segment accounting for all of the growth. Growth in government bond issuance soared by 40.9% q-o-q after falling 4.0% q-o-q in Q1 2022. The surge in government bond issuance was largely driven by higher sales of local

Table 3: Local Currency Bond Issuance (gross)

	Q2 2021		Q1 2022		Q2 2022		Growth Rate (LCY-base %) Q2 2022		Growth Rate (USD-base %) Q2 2022	
	Amount (USD billion)	% share	Amount (USD billion)	% share	Amount (USD billion)	% share	q-o-q	y-o-y	q-o-q	y-o-y
China, People's Rep. of										
Total	1,492	100.0	1,481	100.0	1,629	100.0	16.3	13.3	10.0	9.2
Government	793	53.1	747	50.4	996	61.1	40.9	30.3	33.4	25.6
Central Bank	0	0.0	0	0.0	0	0.0	–	–	–	–
Treasury and Other Govt.	793	53.1	747	50.4	996	61.1	40.9	30.3	33.4	25.6
Corporate	699	46.9	734	49.6	633	38.9	(8.8)	(6.0)	(13.7)	(9.4)
Hong Kong, China										
Total	140	100.0	148	100.0	154	100.0	4.3	10.9	4.1	9.7
Government	110	78.5	120	81.3	122	79.3	1.7	11.9	1.5	10.8
Central Bank	106	75.9	120	81.0	121	78.6	1.1	14.7	0.9	13.5
Treasury and Other Govt.	4	2.6	0.4	0.3	1	0.7	157.6	(69.9)	157.1	(70.2)
Corporate	30	21.5	28	18.7	32	20.7	15.6	7.0	15.4	5.9
Indonesia										
Total	39	100.0	46	100.0	34	100.0	(22.4)	(8.8)	(25.1)	(11.2)
Government	37	96.6	43	94.1	32	94.0	(22.4)	(11.2)	(25.2)	(13.6)
Central Bank	21	55.3	26	57.7	22	65.0	(12.5)	7.2	(15.6)	4.4
Treasury and Other Govt.	16	41.3	17	36.4	10	29.1	(38.1)	(35.9)	(40.3)	(37.6)
Corporate	1	3.4	3	5.9	2	6.0	(21.4)	61.7	(24.2)	57.3
Korea, Rep. of										
Total	235	100.0	193	100.0	190	100.0	5.4	(7.0)	(1.7)	(19.4)
Government	101	43.2	81	42.0	79	41.8	4.9	(9.9)	(2.2)	(21.9)
Central Bank	31	13.3	25	12.9	18	9.6	(21.2)	(32.6)	(26.5)	(41.5)
Treasury and Other Govt.	70	29.9	56	29.1	61	32.2	16.4	0.1	8.6	(13.2)
Corporate	134	56.8	112	58.0	110	58.2	5.7	(4.8)	(1.3)	(17.4)
Malaysia										
Total	24	100.0	19	100.0	25	100.0	35.5	9.0	29.2	2.6
Government	13	55.3	12	61.4	15	60.6	33.7	19.4	27.5	12.3
Central Bank	0	0.0	0	0.0	0.2	0.8	–	–	–	–
Treasury and Other Govt.	13	55.3	12	61.4	15	59.8	32.0	17.9	25.9	10.9
Corporate	11	44.7	7	38.6	10	39.4	38.3	(3.8)	31.9	(9.5)
Philippines										
Total	42	100.0	46	100.0	43	100.0	0.3	15.8	(5.6)	2.8
Government	41	97.7	43	93.6	42	96.2	3.1	14.0	(3.0)	1.2
Central Bank	26	60.8	25	55.6	32	73.1	31.9	39.3	24.2	23.7
Treasury and Other Govt.	16	36.9	17	38.0	10	23.1	(39.1)	(27.7)	(42.7)	(35.8)
Corporate	1	2.3	3	6.4	2	3.8	(40.2)	94.0	(43.7)	72.2
Singapore										
Total	194	100.0	215	100.0	243	100.0	16.1	29.0	13.0	24.9
Government	185	95.4	213	99.2	239	98.5	15.2	33.2	12.2	28.8
Central Bank	155	80.0	187	87.4	209	86.2	14.6	39.1	11.6	34.6
Treasury and Other Govt.	30	15.4	25	11.8	30	12.2	20.1	2.2	17.0	(1.1)
Corporate	9	4.6	2	0.8	4	1.5	113.0	(56.7)	107.5	(58.1)
Thailand										
Total	69	100.0	63	100.0	61	100.0	2.9	(1.7)	(3.2)	(10.9)
Government	54	78.4	50	79.2	44	72.5	(5.9)	(9.1)	(11.5)	(17.6)
Central Bank	35	51.0	34	53.3	25	40.5	(21.8)	(22.0)	(26.4)	(29.2)
Treasury and Other Govt.	19	27.4	16	25.9	20	32.0	26.8	14.7	19.3	4.0
Corporate	15	21.6	13	20.8	17	27.5	36.3	25.1	28.3	13.5

continued on next page

Table 3 *continued*

	Q2 2021		Q1 2022		Q2 2022		Growth Rate (LCY-base %)		Growth Rate (USD-base %)	
							Q2 2022		Q2 2022	
	Amount (USD billion)	% share	Amount (USD billion)	% share	Amount (USD billion)	% share	q-o-q	y-o-y	q-o-q	y-o-y
Viet Nam										
Total	9	100.0	5	100.0	12	100.0	158.5	25.7	153.5	24.2
Government	4	47.7	3	70.0	9	74.4	174.8	96.0	169.5	93.7
Central Bank	0	0.0	1	30.4	7	62.2	429.3	–	419.2	–
Treasury and Other Govt.	4	47.7	2	39.6	1	12.2	(20.5)	(67.9)	(22.1)	(68.3)
Corporate	5	52.3	1	30.0	3	25.6	120.5	(38.4)	116.3	(39.2)
Emerging East Asia										
Total	2,245	100.0	2,215	100.0	2,391	100.0	13.4	11.8	7.9	6.5
Government	1,340	59.7	1,312	59.2	1,578	66.0	25.9	23.4	20.3	17.8
Central Bank	375	16.7	419	18.9	435	18.2	6.5	21.3	3.7	15.8
Treasury and Other Govt.	965	43.0	893	40.3	1,144	47.8	35.3	24.1	28.1	18.5
Corporate	905	40.3	903	40.8	813	34.0	(4.9)	(5.4)	(10.0)	(10.2)
Japan										
Total	505	100.0	463	100.0	412	100.0	(0.8)	(0.3)	(11.0)	(18.4)
Government	462	91.5	444	95.9	384	93.3	(3.5)	1.6	(13.5)	(16.8)
Central Bank	10	1.9	0	0.0	16	3.9	–	107.6	–	69.9
Treasury and Other Govt.	452	89.6	444	95.9	368	89.3	(7.6)	(0.6)	(17.1)	(18.6)
Corporate	43	8.5	19	4.1	28	6.7	61.5	(20.8)	44.8	(35.2)

( ) = negative, – = not applicable, LCY = local currency, q-o-q = quarter-on-quarter, Q1 = first quarter, Q2 = second quarter, USD = United States dollar, y-o-y = year-on-year.
Notes:
1. Corporate bonds include issues by financial institutions.
2. Bloomberg LP end-of-period LCY–USD rates are used.
3. For LCY base, emerging East Asia growth figures are based on 30 June 2022 currency exchange rates and do not include currency effects.
Sources: People's Republic of China (CEIC Data Company); Hong Kong, China (Hong Kong Monetary Authority); Indonesia (Bank Indonesia; Directorate General of Budget Financing and Risk Management, Ministry of Finance; and Indonesia Stock Exchange); Republic of Korea (KG Zeroin Corporation and The Bank of Korea); Malaysia (Bank Negara Malaysia); Philippines (Bureau of the Treasury and Bloomberg LP); Singapore (Singapore Government Securities and Bloomberg LP); Thailand (Bank of Thailand); Viet Nam (Bloomberg LP, Hanoi Stock Exchange, and Vietnam Bond Market Association); and Japan (Japan Securities Dealers Association).

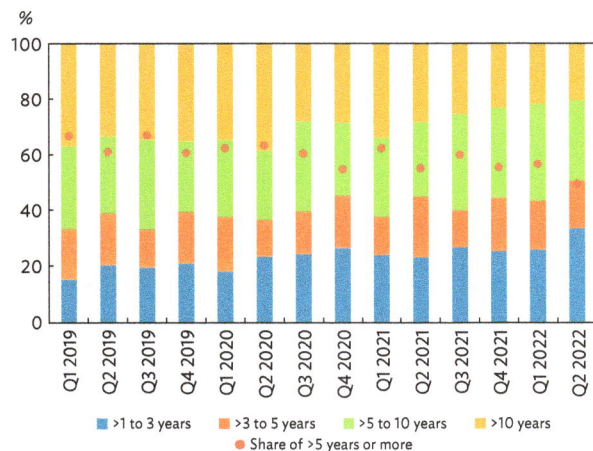

Figure 8: Maturity Structure of Local Currency Government Bond Issuance in Emerging East Asia

Q1 = first quarter, Q2 = second quarter, Q3 = third quarter, Q4 = fourth quarter.
Notes:
1. Emerging East Asia is defined to include Cambodia; the People's Republic of China; Hong Kong, China; Indonesia; the Republic of Korea; the Lao People's Democratic Republic; Malaysia; the Philippines; Singapore; Thailand; and Viet Nam.
2. Figures were computed based on 30 June 2022 currency exchange rates and do not include currency effects.
Source: *AsianBondsOnline* computations based on various local sources.

government bonds during the quarter. The government pushed for the utilization of the entire special bond quota by the end of June to help boost economic and investment activities in response to the impacts of the lockdown restrictions implemented in some major cities in the PRC in March and April. The special bond issuance quota, which was set at CNY3.65 trillion for 2022, was almost fully utilized, as issuance for January to June reached about CNY3.40 trillion. Funds raised from special bond issuances need to either be spent or allocated for projects by August.

Issuance of Treasury bonds climbed 16.3% q-o-q in Q2 2022 on the increased financing needs of the government to support stimulus and recovery measures. Policy bank bond issuance also grew 5.2% q-o-q during the quarter. Amid property default and economic growth concerns that continued to cloud the outlook for the PRC bond market, corporate bond issuance declined 8.8% q-o-q in Q2 2022. On a y-o-y basis, LCY bond issuance growth in the PRC eased to 13.3% in Q2 2022 from 14.2% in Q1 2022.

In the Republic of Korea, LCY bond issuance rose 5.4% q-o-q in Q2 2022, reversing the 4.0% q-o-q decline in the prior quarter. Total issuance reached USD189.6 billion, with growth driven by Treasury and other government bonds and corporate bonds. Growth in the government bond segment was capped by the 21.2% q-o-q contraction in the issuance of central bank instruments as the Bank of Korea opted to further tighten monetary policy by raising its policy rate five times between January and August to rein in surging inflation. Treasury and other government bonds climbed 16.4% q-o-q as the government continued with its frontloading policy of issuance. Corporate bond issuance also rebounded in Q2 2022 on growth of 5.7% q-o-q following a 21.1% q-o-q decline in Q1 2022. Compared with the same period a year earlier, LCY bond issuance in the Republic of Korea contracted 7.0% y-o-y in Q2 2022 after marginal growth of 0.8% y-o-y in Q1 2022.

LCY bond sales in Hong Kong, China climbed to USD153.8 billion in Q2 2022, with growth inching up to 4.3% q-o-q from 3.1% q-o-q in the preceding quarter. Both major bond segments contributed to the increased issuance volume during the quarter, led by corporate bonds. Corporate bond issuance totaled USD31.8 billion, up 15.6% q-o-q, as corporates rushed to issue bonds amid rising interest rates. Issuance of EFBs and EFNs reached USD120.9 billion, with growth moderating to 1.1% q-o-q in Q2 2022 from 3.0% q-o-q in Q1 2022. Issuance of EFBs and EFNs accounted for 78.6% of Hong Kong, China's aggregate issuance during the quarter. Issuance of Hong Kong Special Administrative Region bonds more than doubled during the quarter, which included the first issuance of a 20-year maturity. On a y-o-y basis, LCY bond issuance in Hong Kong, China surged to 10.9% in Q2 2022 from 4.0% in Q1 2022.

Aggregate LCY bond issuance among ASEAN members rose to USD418.1 billion in Q2 2022. Overall growth rebounded, rising 10.3% q-o-q in Q2 2022 after contracting 6.9% q-o-q in the preceding quarter. Over the same period, issuance growth eased to 16.9% y-o-y from 19.6% y-o-y. Five out of six ASEAN member economies increased their issuance of LCY bonds during the quarter. The sole exception was Indonesia, which continued to reduce its borrowings in the LCY bond market. Among ASEAN members, the largest bond issuance totals were in Singapore, Thailand, and the Philippines, representing 58.0%, 14.7%, and 10.4%, respectively, of the ASEAN issuance total during the quarter.

LCY bond issuance in Singapore climbed to USD242.6 billion in Q2 2022, rising 16.1% q-o-q following a decline of 11.7% q-o-q in Q1 2022. Central bank bonds, which accounted for a majority of the issuance total, rose 14.6% q-o-q in Q2 2022, a turnaround from the 10.6% q-o-q drop in the prior quarter. Treasury and other government bond issuance grew 20.1% q-o-q, albeit its contribution to the overall issuance total is much less. Corporate bond issuance also picked up during the quarter, with volumes more than doubling from Q1 2022. Compared with the same period a year earlier, Singapore's LCY bond issuance inched up to 29.0% y-o-y in Q2 2022 from 28.2% y-o-y in Q1 2022.

LCY bond issuance in Thailand totaled USD61.4 billion as growth eased to 2.9% q-o-q in Q2 2022 from 3.2% q-o-q in Q1 2022. Overall growth was dragged down by the 21.8% q-o-q decline in the issuance of central bank instruments, which accounted for 40.5% of Thailand's total issuance during the quarter. The BOT reduced its issuance of debt instruments to help maintain market liquidity as global financial conditions weakened. Meanwhile, issuance of Treasury and other government bonds rose 26.8% q-o-q, buoyed by the issuance of Retail Treasury Bonds in June. The government raised THB52.7 billion from the bond sale comprising 5-year and 10-year maturities offered to individuals and nonprofit entities. Corporate bond issuance climbed 36.3% q-o-q in the same period. On a y-o-y basis, LCY bond issuance in Thailand declined 1.7% in Q2 2022 after 6.4% growth in the preceding quarter.

In the Philippines, issuance of LCY bonds grew a marginal 0.3% q-o-q to reach USD43.3 billion. The sole driver of growth was central bank issuance, which rose 31.9% q-o-q. The Bangko Sentral ng Pilipinas was quite active in the issuance of bills during the quarter amid rising inflationary pressure. Issuance of Treasury and other government bonds declined 39.1% q-o-q in Q2 2022 due to a high-base effect from the previous quarter following the issuance of Retail Treasury Bonds in March. Corporate bond issuance also slowed, falling 40.2% q-o-q. On an annual basis, the Philippines' LCY bond issuance growth accelerated to 15.8% y-o-y in Q2 2022 from 10.9% y-o-y in Q1 2022.

Indonesia was the only market in the region that tapered its issuance volume across all bond segments in Q2 2022. Total issuance slipped to USD34.3 billion in Q2 2022 on a contraction of 22.4% q-o-q, which followed a 5.3% q-o-q drop in the prior quarter. Treasury and other government bond issuance, which accounted for 29.1% of the total issuance volume during the quarter, fell the most with a decline of 38.1% q-o-q. The slowdown in issuance is in line with the government's plan to reduce bond issuance in full-year 2022. Strong government revenues arising from higher commodity prices and increased exports are projected to result in a smaller budget deficit for the year, allowing the government to reduce bond issuance. The budget deficit is estimated to reach 3.9% of GDP, down from an earlier estimate of 4.5%. The Ministry of Finance is looking at reducing its total bond issuance in 2022 to IDR757.6 trillion from IDR943.7 trillion as earlier planned. Issuance of central bank instruments also declined during the quarter as inflation in Indonesia remained modest relative to regional peers. Corporate bond issuance fell 21.4% q-o-q, a turnaround from a 24.0% q-o-q hike in Q1 2022. On a y-o-y basis, LCY bond issuance in Indonesia fell 8.8% in Q2 2022 versus 31.6% y-o-y growth in Q1 2022.

LCY bond sales in Malaysia tallied USD25.0 billion in Q2 2022 on growth of 35.5% q-o-q. Growth was broadly at par between the government and corporate bond segments. Government bond issuance growth in Malaysia accelerated to 33.7% q-o-q in Q2 2022 from 4.5% q-o-q in Q1 2022 to refinance maturing obligations and to fund increased subsidies to mitigate the impact of rising commodity prices. Central bank issuance also resumed during the quarter since the last issuance by BNM in Q2 2020, albeit only USD0.2 billion worth of bills. Corporate bond issuance also rose 38.3% q-o-q in Q2 2022 after falling 23.7% q-o-q in the prior quarter ahead of an anticipated hike in funding costs. On a y-o-y basis, overall issuance grew 9.0% in Q2 2022.

In Viet Nam, LCY bond issuance more than doubled to reach USD11.6 billion in Q2 2022. Overall growth surged to 158.5% q-o-q in Q2 2022 on increased issuance of central bank bills and corporate bonds. Issuance of Treasury and other government bonds, on the other hand, contracted 20.5% q-o-q. On a y-o-y basis, LCY bond issuance growth moderated to 25.7% in Q2 2022 from 80.4% in Q1 2022.

Cross-Border Bond Issuance

Emerging East Asia's cross-border bond issuance reached USD7.0 billion in Q2 2022.

Emerging East Asia's cross-border bond issuance totaled USD7.0 billion in Q2 2022, a 20.3% q-o-q decline from the USD8.7 billion raised in the previous quarter. The lower issuance volume for the quarter may be attributed to increased volatility in global yields following a series of Federal Reserve rate hikes since March. Institutions from five economies raised funds via cross-border bond issuance in Q2 2022, a grouping that was once again largely dominated by firms from Hong Kong, China (**Figure 9**). Other economies that registered cross-border bond issuance during the quarter included the Republic of Korea, Singapore, the PRC, and Malaysia. Monthly issuance volumes amounted to USD3.1 billion, USD1.3 billion, and USD2.6 billion in April, May, and June, respectively. Compared with Q2 2021, cross-border bond issuance posted a marginal decline of 3.8% y-o-y from USD7.3 billion.

Hong Kong, China continued to register the largest issuance volume in the region in Q2 2022 as it is home to the most developed bond market infrastructure, which makes it more accessible and efficient for companies to issue cross-border bonds. Total cross-border bond issuance from firms based in Hong Kong, China amounted to USD5.2 billion in Q2 2022, a 23.5% q-o-q decline from the USD6.8 billion raised in the previous quarter.

Figure 9: Origin Economies of Intra-Emerging East Asian Bond Issuance in the Second Quarter of 2022

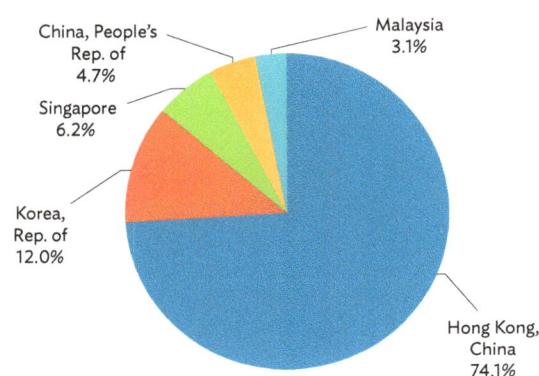

China, People's Rep. of 4.7%
Singapore 6.2%
Korea, Rep. of 12.0%
Malaysia 3.1%
Hong Kong, China 74.1%

Source: *AsianBondsOnline* calculations based on Bloomberg LP data.

Fourteen firms issued cross-border bonds in Q2 2022, all of which were denominated in Chinese yuan. Institutions from the transportation and finance sectors led the issuances in terms of volume, with shares of 41.9% and 24.3%, respectively. China Merchants Group, a PRC state-owned company based in Hong Kong, China and primarily involved in shipping and integrated transportation, was the largest cross-border bond issuer in the region in Q2 2022. China Merchants Group raised a total of USD2.1 billion comprising short-term bonds (CNY10.0 billion) and perpetual bonds (CNY4.0 billion). China Power International, another PRC state-owned company, was the second-largest issuer with an aggregate issuance volume of USD746.3 million. The Hong Kong Mortgage Corporation followed with a total of USD668.4 million via issuance of multitranche bonds. China Everbright Limited and China Tourism were the other notable issuers in Hong Kong, China with issuance volumes of USD447.8 million each.

In the Republic of Korea, three banks issued cross-border bonds in Q2 2022 with an aggregate issuance volume of USD837.8 million. State-owned Korea Development Bank was the largest issuer at USD645.3 million. The state bank issued multiple bonds during the quarter, denominated in both Chinese yuan and Hong Kong dollars, with tenors of 1–10 years. The other two banks that issued cross-border bonds during the quarter were Industrial Bank of Korea (USD162.7 million) and Kookmin Bank (USD29.9 million), all of which were denominated in Chinese yuan.

In Singapore, five institutions issued cross-border bonds in Q2 2022 with an aggregate volume of USD429.3 million. PSA Treasury Pte., a port and harbor operator, led the issuances with USD159.3 million worth of 10-year bonds denominated in Hong Kong dollars. The two other major issuers in Singapore included United Overseas Bank (USD97.0 million) and Singtel Group (USD95.6 million).

Property company CIFI Holdings Group was the sole issuer of cross-border bonds in the PRC, raising USD324.4 million via HKD-denominated 3-year bonds. In Malaysia, Malayan Banking was the sole issuer and raised USD214.9 million via 1-year and 3-year CNY-denominated bonds.

The top 10 issuers of cross-border bonds in Q2 2022 had an aggregate issuance volume of USD6.1 billion and accounted for 87.4% of the regional total.

Seven firms were from Hong Kong, China, led by China Merchants and China Power International. The other three firms were from the Republic of Korea (Korea Development Bank), the PRC (CIFI Holdings), and Malaysia (Malayan Banking).

The Chinese yuan continued to be the most widely used currency for cross-border bonds in the region in Q2 2022, with an aggregate issuance volume of USD6.1 billion and a market share of 87.2% (**Figure 10**). Firms from Hong Kong, China; the Republic of Korea; Malaysia; and Singapore issued in this currency. Other currencies used for cross-border bond issuances in Q2 2022 include the Hong Kong dollar (11.7%, USD814.8 million) and Malaysian ringgit (1.1%, USD77.1 million).

In Q2 2022, the financial sector remained the most active issuer of cross-border bonds in emerging East Asia, with an aggregate volume of USD2.5 billion and a 35.6% share of the regional cross-border issuance total (**Figure 11**). The two largest issuers from this sector were the Hong Kong Mortgage Corporation (USD668.4 million) and the Korea Development Bank (USD645.2 million). The transportation sector was the next largest, with aggregate issuance volume of USD2.2 billion comprising 31.0% of the regional total. Two firms from Hong Kong, China accounted for all of the cross-border bond issuance in this sector, China Merchants Group (USD2.1 billion) and Yuexiu Transport (USD74.6 million). The utilities sector registered the largest percentage increase to 10.7% from 3.9% compared with the previous

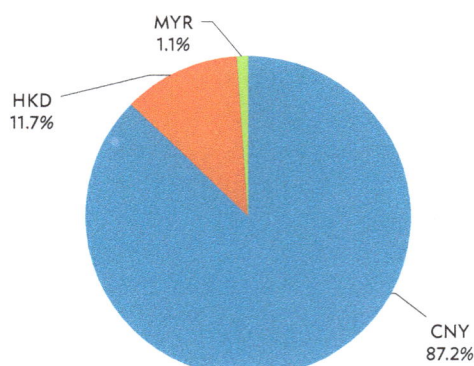

Figure 10: Currency Shares of Intra-Emerging East Asian Bond Issuance in the Second Quarter of 2022

MYR 1.1%
HKD 11.7%
CNY 87.2%

CNY = Chinese yuan, HKD = Hong Kong dollar, MYR = Malaysian ringgit.
Source: *AsianBondsOnline* calculations based on Bloomberg LP data.

Figure 11: Intra-Emerging East Asian Bond Issuance by Sector

USD billion

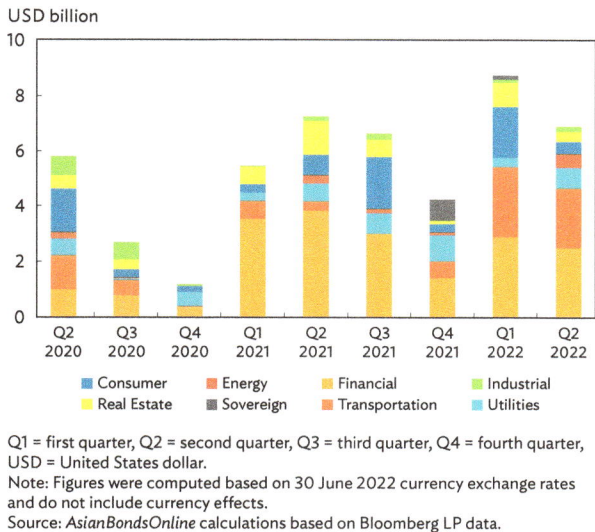

Q1 = first quarter, Q2 = second quarter, Q3 = third quarter, Q4 = fourth quarter, USD = United States dollar.
Note: Figures were computed based on 30 June 2022 currency exchange rates and do not include currency effects.
Source: *AsianBondsOnline* calculations based on Bloomberg LP data.

quarter. Other sectors that registered cross-border bond issuance in Q2 2022 were energy, consumer, real estate, industrial, and communications.

G3 Currency Bond Issuance

Emerging East Asia's G3 currency bond issuance from January to July amounted to USD165.7 billion.

Emerging East Asian economies issued G3 currency bonds during January–July amounting to USD165.7 billion, a decline of 33.1% y-o-y from January–July 2021's total of USD247.5 billion (**Table 4**).[4] Among all economies in the region, only Thailand recorded a higher volume of G3 currency issuance during the review period on increased issuance by financial institutions. All other emerging East Asian economies logged large declines as it became more expensive to raise funds in G3 currencies, largely due to Federal Reserve rate hikes and the appreciation of the US dollar versus regional currencies.

In the first 7 months of 2022, 93.2% of the total G3 currency bonds issued by emerging East Asian entities were denominated in US dollars, 5.8% in euros, and 1.0% in Japanese yen. USD-denominated bonds

totaled USD154.5 billion during the January–July period, a decline of 33.3% y-o-y from January–July 2021 on sluggish issuance activity from all economies in emerging East Asia except for Thailand. Issuance of EUR-denominated bonds totaled USD9.6 billion during the review period, a contraction of 32.4% y-o-y, as issuances from the PRC declined and there was an absence of issuance from most other regional markets. Samurai bonds, which are denominated in Japanese yen, totaled USD1.6 billion during the first 7 months of 2022, shrinking 7.6% y-o-y due to a drop in issuance from Indonesia and Hong Kong, China, while Singapore had no G3 currency issuance during the review period.

Entities from the PRC continued to dominate the region in terms of G3 currency bonds issued, raising the equivalent of USD98.7 billion in January–July 2022. The Republic of Korea came next with USD27.9 billion, followed by Hong Kong, China with USD11.6 billion. All issuers in emerging East Asia chose the US dollar as their main currency in their G3 currency fundraising activities during the review period.

An annual drop in G3 currency bond issuance from January to July was posted in nearly all economies in the region: the Philippines (–63.4%); Malaysia (–60.5%); Hong Kong, China (–59.9%); Indonesia (–57.7%); the PRC (–26.9%); Singapore (–9.8%); and the Republic of Korea (–7.4%). Only Thailand posted an expansion with a 4.3% y-o-y growth. Viet Nam did not issue any G3 currency bonds from January to July 2022 after issuing G3 currency bonds during the same period in the preceding year.

From January to July 2022, 59.6% of all emerging East Asian G3 currency bond sales came from the PRC: USD93.1 billion in US dollars, the equivalent of USD5.4 billion in euros, and the equivalent of USD0.2 billion in Japanese yen. In May, NXP BV/NXP Funding issued 12 USD-denominated callable bonds with tenors ranging from 3 to 30 years and totaling USD9.2 billion. The most notable among them was the 11-year bond with a periodic distribution rate of 5.0%. The proceeds from this bond will be used to fund the global semiconductor company's green projects. In July, Easy Tactic issued a triple-tranche USD-denominated callable bond totaling USD5.1 billion—with tenors of 3 years, 5 years, and 6 years—and the same coupon rate of

---

[4] G3 currency bonds are denominated in either euros, Japanese yen, or US dollars. For the discussion on G3 currency issuance, emerging East Asia comprises the People's Republic of China; Hong Kong, China; Indonesia; the Republic of Korea; Malaysia; the Philippines; Singapore; Thailand; and Viet Nam.

Table 4: G3 Currency Bond Issuance

2021			January–July 2022		
Issuer	Amount (USD billion)	Issue Date	Issuer	Amount (USD billion)	Issue Date
China, People's Rep. of	**217.4**		**China, People's Rep. of**	**98.7**	
Industrial and Commercial Bank of China 3.200% Perpetual	6.2	24-Sep-21	Easy Tactic 7.50% 2027	2.2	11-Jul-22
China Development Bank 0.380% 2022	2.0	10-Jun-21	China Construction Bank 2.85% 2032	2.0	21-Jan-22
Prosus 3.061% 2031	1.9	13-Jul-21	Easy Tactic 7.50% 2028	1.6	11-Jul-22
Others	207.4		Others	92.9	
Hong Kong, China	**39.7**		**Hong Kong, China**	**11.6**	
Hong Kong, China (Sovereign) 0.000% 2026	1.4	24-Nov-21	Airport Authority Hong Kong 2.50% 2032	1.2	12-Jan-22
NWD Finance 4.125% Perpetual	1.2	10-Jun-21	Airport Authority Hong Kong 3.25% 2052	1.2	12-Jan-22
Hong Kong, China (Sovereign) 0.625% 2026	1.0	2-Feb-21	Airport Authority Hong Kong 1.75% 2027	1.0	12-Jan-22
Others	36.1		Others	8.2	
Indonesia	**26.4**		**Indonesia**	**8.9**	
Indonesia (Sovereign) 3.05% 2051	2.0	12-Jan-21	Perusahaan Penerbit SBSN Indonesia III 4.400% 2027	1.8	6-Jun-22
Perusahaan Penerbit SBSN Indonesia III 1.50% 2026	1.3	9-Jun-21	Perusahaan Penerbit SBSN Indonesia III 4.700% 2032	1.5	6-Jun-22
Indonesia (Sovereign) 1.85% 2031	1.3	12-Jan-21	Freeport Indonesia 5.315% 2032	1.5	14-Apr-22
Others	21.9		Others	4.1	
Korea, Rep. of	**43.9**		**Korea, Rep. of**	**27.9**	
Posco 0.00% 2026	1.2	1-Sep-21	Export–Import Bank of Korea 1.250% 2025	1.0	18-Jan-22
Korea Housing Finance Corporation 0.01% 2026	1.1	29-Jun-21	Korea Development Bank 2.000% 2025	1.0	24-Feb-22
SK Hynix 1.50% 2026	1.0	19-Jan-21	Export-Import Bank of Korea 1.625% 2027	1.0	18-Jan-22
Others	40.6		Others	24.9	
Malaysia	**16.0**		**Malaysia**	**4.8**	
Petronas Capital 3.404% 2061	1.8	28-Apr-21	Misc Capital Two (Labuan) 3.75% 2027	0.6	6-Apr-22
Petronas Capital 2.480% 2032	1.3	28-Apr-21	Bank Negara Malaysia 0.00% 2022	0.6	25-Jan-22
Others	13.0		Others	3.6	
Philippines	**10.8**		**Philippines**	**2.8**	
Philippines (Sovereign) 3.200% 2046	2.3	6-Jul-21	Philippines (Sovereign) 4.200% 2047	1.0	29-Mar-22
Philippines (Sovereign) 1.375% 2026	1.1	8-Oct-21	Philippines (Sovereign) 3.556% 2032	0.8	29-Mar-22
Others	7.5		Others	1.0	
Singapore	**16.5**		**Singapore**	**8.7**	
BOC Aviation 1.625% 2024	1.0	29-Apr-21	United Overseas Bank 0.387% 2025	1.5	17-Mar-22
Temasek Financial I 2.750% 2061	1.0	2-Aug-21	DBS Bank 2.375% 2027	1.5	17-Mar-22
Others	14.5		Others	5.7	
Thailand	**4.1**		**Thailand**	**2.4**	
Bangkok Bank in Hong Kong, China 3.466% 2036	1.0	23-Sep-21	GC Treasury Center 4.4% 2032	1.0	30-Mar-22
GC Treasury Center 2.980% 2031	0.7	18-Mar-21	Bangkok Bank in Hong Kong, China 4.3% 2027	0.8	15-Jun-22
Others	2.4		Others	0.7	
Viet Nam	**1.6**		**Viet Nam**	**–**	
Emerging East Asia Total	**376.4**		**Emerging East Asia Total**	**165.7**	
Memo Items:			Memo Items:		
India	**23.7**		**India**	**6.8**	
Vedanta Resources 8.95% 2025	1.2	11-Mar-21	Reliance Industries 3.625% 2052	1.8	12-Jan-22
Others	22.5		Others	5.1	
Sri Lanka	**0.8**		**Sri Lanka**	**0.01**	
Sri Lanka (Sovereign) 7.95% 2024	0.2	3-May-21	Sri Lanka (Sovereign) 8% 2023	0.01	24-Jan-22
Others	**0.6**		Others	**0.0006**	

USD = United States dollar.
Notes:
1.   Data exclude certificates of deposit.
2.   G3 currency bonds are bonds denominated in either euros, Japanese yen, or US dollars.
3.   Bloomberg LP end-of-period rates are used.
4.   Emerging East Asia is defined to include Cambodia; the People's Republic of China; Hong Kong, China; Indonesia; the Republic of Korea; the Lao People's Democratic Republic; Malaysia; the Philippines; Singapore. Thailand; and Viet Nam.
5.   Figures after the issuer name reflect the coupon rate and year of maturity of the bond.
Source: *AsianBondsOnline* calculations based on Bloomberg LP data.

7.5%. The issuance was part of the real estate developer's debt restructuring wherein 10 outstanding bonds were consolidated into the three tranches of the issuance.

Entities from the Republic of Korea accounted for a 16.9% share of all G3 currency bond issuances from the region during the review period: USD25.3 billion was raised in US dollars and the equivalent of USD2.6 billion was raised in euros. From May to July, Kookmin Bank issued nine USD-denominated bonds with tenors of 1–5 years for an aggregate total of USD601.0 million. Toward the end of June, the bank also issued a 4-year EUR-denominated sustainability mortgage-backed bond worth USD511.0 million. Proceeds from the bond will be used to finance new and existing loans. Another prolific issuer during the May–July period was Shinhan Bank, which issued 16 bonds denominated in US dollars with tenors of 1–5 years totaling USD645.0 million.

Hong Kong, China accounted for a regional share of 7.0% of bond issuances denominated in G3 currencies from January to July 2022, comprising USD-denominated bonds totaling USD11.5 billion and JPY-denominated bonds amounting to USD0.1 billion. In June and July, the Hong Kong Mortgage Corporation issued various bonds denominated in US dollars totaling USD680.0 million. The issuances had tenors ranging from 3 months to 5 years and coupon rates of 2.20% to 3.31%. In July, the Bank of East Asia raised USD250.0 million from a 6-year callable USD-denominated bond, the proceeds of which will be used for general corporate purposes.

During the first 7 months of the year, the G3 currency bond issuance of ASEAN member economies fell 48.7% y-o-y.[5] Only USD27.5 billion worth of G3 currency bonds were issued by ASEAN members, well below the USD53.6 billion issuance logged in the first 7 months of 2021, as all member economies except for Thailand slowed their fundraising activities. During the review period, issuance of ASEAN member economies had a regional share of 16.6% of the total issuance of G3 currency bonds, falling from 21.7% in the previous year. In January–July 2022, Indonesia had the most G3 currency bond issuance among ASEAN members, followed by Singapore, Malaysia, the Philippines, and Thailand.

In the January–July review period, Indonesian G3 currency bond issuance comprised 5.4% of the emerging East Asian total. A majority of the issuances were denominated in US dollars totaling USD8.3 billion. A small portion, USD0.6 billion worth, was denominated in Japanese yen. In June, Perusahaan Penerbit SBSN Indonesia III, a special purpose vehicle of the Government of Indonesia, issued a dual-tranche *sukuk* denominated in US dollars. With tenors of 5 years and 10 years, the issuance totaled USD3.3 billion. In the same month, the Government of Indonesia raised the equivalent of USD607.8 million from four tranches of samurai bonds with tenors of 3–10 years. Proceeds from the JPY-denominated debenture will be used to address the government's budget deficit.

Singapore had a 5.2% share of emerging East Asia's G3 currency bond issuance total during the review period, issuing USD7.1 billion in US dollars and the equivalent of USD1.6 billion in euros. In May, Singapore Technologies Engineering Urban Solutions issued a dual-tranche callable bond denominated in US dollars totaling USD1.0 billion. The issuance with tenors of 5 years and 10 years was drawn from the technology company's global medium-term note program. In June, Oversea-Chinese Banking Corporation sold USD750.0 million worth of 10-year USD-denominated callable bonds. Proceeds from the issuance will be used for the bank's general corporate purposes.

The G3 currency bond issuance of Malaysian entities comprised 2.9% of the emerging East Asia total. Issuances of USD-denominated bonds reached USD4.6 billion, while JPY-denominated bonds amounted to USD0.2 billion. From May to July, the BNM issued several zero-coupon Bank Negara Interbank Bills denominated in US dollars totaling USD1.2 billion. Toward the end of July, Malayan Banking raised USD30.0 million from a USD-denominated, 5-year floating-rate bond from the bank's multicurrency medium-term note program.

The first 7 months of 2022 saw the Philippines accounting for a 1.7% share of the emerging East Asian G3 currency bond issuance total. By currency, Philippine entities issued USD2.3 billion worth of bonds denominated in US dollars and the equivalent of USD0.5 billion in Japanese yen. All of these issuances occurred on March and April.

---

[5] For the discussion on G3 currency issuance, data for ASEAN include Indonesia, Malaysia, the Philippines, Singapore, Thailand, and Viet Nam.

Thailand had a share of 1.4% of all G3 currency bond issuances from emerging East Asia during the January–July period, with fundraising activities from USD-denominated bonds amounting to USD2.4 billion. In June, Bangkok Bank in Hong Kong, China and the Export–Import Bank of Thailand each issued 5-year USD-denominated bonds worth USD750.0 million and USD350.0 million, respectively. Proceeds from both bonds will be used for general corporate purposes.

Figure 12 presents monthly G3 currency bond sales of emerging East Asia from July 2021 to July 2022. Issuances trended down after April 2022, following the series of rate hikes by the Federal Reserve. The decline in May was driven by reduced issuance from Hong Kong, China; Malaysia; and Singapore. Entities in Indonesia and the Philippines opted not to issue any G3 currency bonds in May. Even as most economies increased their issuance volumes in June, the regional total was dragged by reduced issuance from the PRC. In July, the increased issuance from the PRC was not enough to lift the region's total as entities from Hong Kong, China and Indonesia limited their issuances, while there was zero G3 currency issuance from Singapore and Thailand during the month.

Figure 12: G3 Currency Bond Issuance in Emerging East Asia

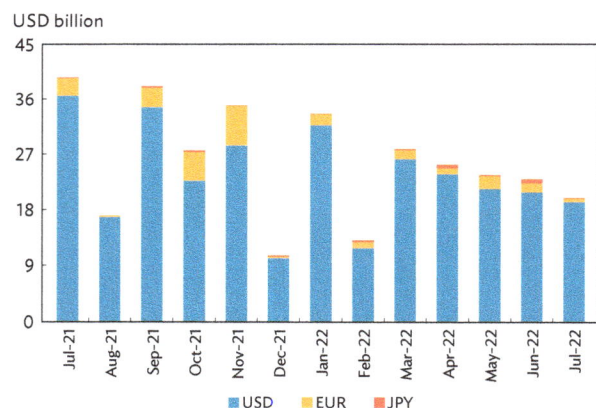

EUR = euro, JPY = Japanese yen, USD = United States dollar.
Notes:
1. Emerging East Asia is defined to include Cambodia; the People's Republic of China; Hong Kong, China; Indonesia; the Republic of Korea; the Lao People's Democratic Republic; Malaysia; the Philippines; Singapore; Thailand; and Viet Nam.
2. Figures were computed based on 31 July 2022 currency exchange rates and do not include currency effects.
Source: *AsianBondsOnline* calculations based on Bloomberg LP data.

Bond Yield Movements

Yields in most emerging East Asian markets fell on expectations that the Federal Reserve would be less aggressive in its monetary tightening.

Inflation continues to rise in the global economy, which has led most central banks to tighten monetary policy in response. The Federal Reserve has been particularly aggressive among advanced economy central banks, which has resulted in an overall tightening of global financial conditions.

Markets were concerned when inflation in the US rose to a 40-year high of 9.1% y-o-y in June. This led to some speculation that the Federal Reserve would become even more aggressive and accelerate its monetary policy tightening. Markets collectively breathed a sigh of relief when the Federal Reserve raised policy rates by 75 bps during its 26–27 July meeting.

Market pressure eased further on indications that global inflation might be tapering. Oil prices have been steadily declining since early June. In the US, there were some signs of inflation peaking as growth in the Consumer Price Index fell to 8.5% y-o-y in July. In addition, July producer prices declined 0.5% month-on-month. While economic growth in the US has been weak, with GDP falling an annualized 0.6% in Q2 2022 after a decline of 1.6% in Q1 2022, the Federal Reserve is not yet especially concerned, noting that the labor market remains strong.

While the Federal Reserve had been the most aggressive advanced economy central bank in terms of responding to inflationary pressures in the first half of 2022, the European Central Bank (ECB) has become more aggressive recently, raising its policy rates by 50 bps on 27 July, which was more than the previously indicated 25 bps increase. The ECB judged that a larger interest rate hike was necessary due to inflationary pressure. Unlike in the US, inflation in the euro area did not ease in July and instead rose to 8.9% y-o-y from 8.6% y-o-y in June. In August, inflation further rose to 9.1% y-o-y. GDP growth also slowed to 3.9% y-o-y in Q2 2022 from 5.4% y-o-y in Q1 2022. During its monetary policy meeting, the ECB unveiled its Transmission Protection Instrument, a new facility that allows it to selectively purchase the government bonds of members in the euro area, to help fine-tune its monetary policy.

The Bank of Japan remained the lone advanced economy central bank holdout, choosing to leave its monetary policy mostly unchanged at its 21 July meeting. While inflation has risen in Japan in 2022, it has not approached the levels seen in the US and euro area. Inflation rose to 2.6% y-o-y in July from 2.4% y-o-y in June. In addition, Japan's GDP expanded 3.5% y-o-y in Q2 2022 after growth of only 0.2% y-o-y in Q1 2022.

Most emerging East Asian yields peaked at the start of the second week of July before trending downward. Concerns about the record-setting inflation reading in the US in June eased after indications from the Federal Reserve that it would stick to the expected 75 bps rate hike, which was subsequently borne out during its 26–27 July meeting.

With concerns about the Federal Reserve's actions abating, yields in most emerging East Asian economies began trending downward in July. A notable exception was the PRC, where the 2-year yield has consistently trended downward since November 2020 (**Figure 13a**), largely due to ongoing weakness in the PRC's economy. The other exceptions were Indonesia, the Philippines, and Viet Nam, whose 2-year yields trended upward between 15 June and 15 August (**Figure 13b**). Yields for shorter tenors in the Philippines were elevated following an off-cycle rate hike by the Philippine central bank. In the case of Indonesia and Viet Nam, 2-year yields rose as both markets optimized the use of open market operations to keep rates elevated. Emerging East Asia's 10-year yield largely followed its

2-year counterpart. In both Hong Kong, China and Singapore, on the other hand, the decline was much more pronounced for the 10-year yield than for the 2-year yield, which spiked in both markets in July and in August (**Figure 14a**). Yields in Hong Kong, China and Singapore largely tracked US yields, where the yield curve remained elevated at the shorter-end due to Federal Reserve rate hikes, while longer-term US yields have fallen on easing inflation expectations. In the Philippines, the 10-year yield fell during the review period, in contrast to its 2-year yield, following easing inflation expectations globally (**Figure 14b**).

Previous monetary tightening in advanced economies and in the region, coupled with easing inflation expectations in the US, led to an overall flattening of yield curves in emerging East Asia from 15 June to 15 August (**Figure 15**). As markets increasingly expect the Federal Reserve to be less aggressive, yields on longer tenors have declined. Yields on the shorter-end, however, either rose or remained relatively elevated as past monetary actions raised interest rates, particularly shorter-term interest rates, and directly affected the short-end of the government yield curve. This also led to a decline in the 10-year over 2-year yield spread in nearly all emerging East Asian markets except for the PRC (**Figure 16**).

While most markets saw elevated interest rates at the shorter-end of the curve and falling longer-term yields, yields declined across all tenors in the PRC on slowing economic growth, shifting the yield curve downward.

Figure 13a: 2-Year Local Currency Government Bond Yields

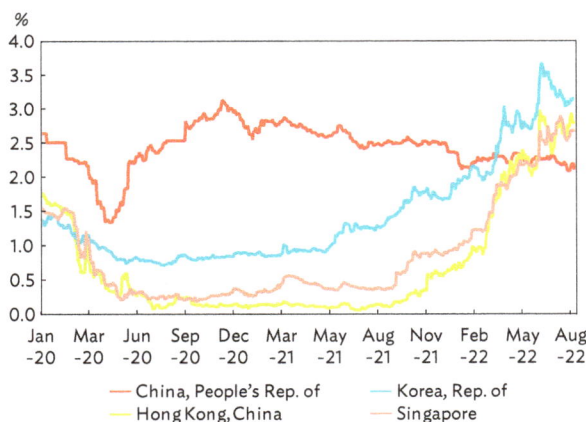

Note: Data coverage is from 1 January 2020 to 15 August 2022.
Source: Based on data from Bloomberg LP.

Figure 13b: 2-Year Local Currency Government Bond Yields

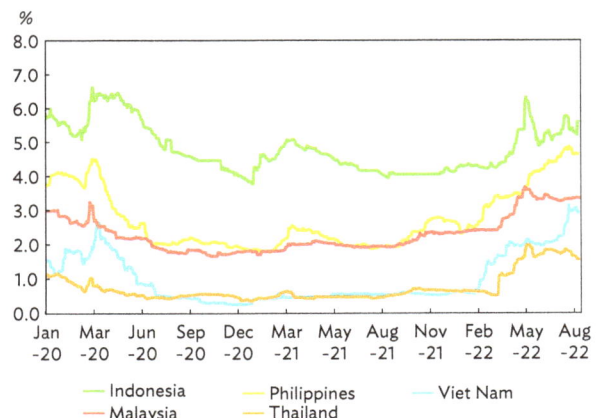

Note: Data coverage is from 1 January 2020 to 15 August 2022.
Source: Based on data from Bloomberg LP.

Figure 14a: 10-Year Local Currency Government Bond Yields

Note: Data coverage is from 1 January 2020 to 15 August 2022.
Source: Based on data from Bloomberg LP.

Figure 14b: 10-Year Local Currency Government Bond Yields

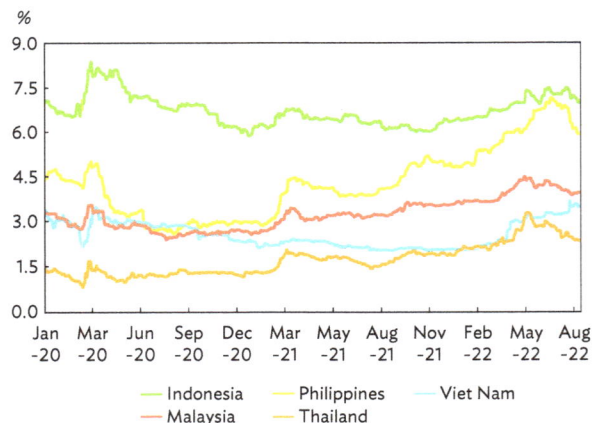

Note: Data coverage is from 1 January 2020 to 15 August 2022.
Source: Based on data from Bloomberg LP.

The PRC's GDP barely grew in Q2 2022, rising only 0.4% y-o-y after gaining 4.8% y-o-y in the previous quarter. The slowdown led the government to announce a slew of stimulus measures at the end of May, including tax rebates and reductions for some industries, and a deferral of social security premium payments.

In contrast with other regional markets, Viet Nam's entire yield curve shifted upward. Viet Nam's economy grew rapidly in Q2 2022, expanding 7.7% y-o-y after growth of 5.0% y-o-y in Q1 2022. The outlook for the economy is positive, with Viet Nam's Ministry of Planning and Investment revising its full-year 2022 growth target to 7.0% from 6.0%–6.5% previously. In addition, while Viet Nam's central bank has not yet adjusted its policy rates this year, it indirectly raised interest rates through open market operations. This had a more direct impact on shorter-term interest rates, which led to a much larger uptick compared to longer-term rates.

Most emerging East Asian economies showed improved growth in Q2 2022. Indonesia's economy expanded 5.4% y-o-y after gaining 5.0% y-o-y in the prior quarter, while Malaysia posted strong growth of 8.9% y-o-y in Q2 2022, up from 5.0% y-o-y in Q1 2022. Singapore's GDP gained 4.4% y-o-y in Q2 2022 after rising 3.8% y-o-y in Q1 2022. Thailand's growth acceleration was less pronounced, with its GDP expanding 2.5% y-o-y in Q2 2022 versus 2.3% y-o-y in Q1 2022.

The region's remaining markets experienced either a contraction or slowing growth in Q2 2022. Hong Kong, China's GDP continued to contract in Q2 2022, dragged down by supply chain disruptions and the impact of COVID-19 containment measures. The Republic of Korea's GDP growth slowed to 2.9% y-o-y in Q2 2022 from 3.0% y-o-y in Q1 2022, while in the Philippines growth eased to 7.4% y-o-y from 8.2% y-o-y during the same period.

Inflation remained elevated in emerging East Asia, trending upward in most markets. Some markets, such as Thailand and Viet Nam, recently recorded slowing inflation (**Figure 17a**). However, Thailand still had the highest inflation rate in the region in July at 7.6% y-o-y. This was followed by Singapore (7.0% y-o-y), the Philippines (6.4% y-o-y), and the Republic of Korea (6.3% y-o-y), which experienced steadily rising inflation during the review period (**Figure 17b**).

High inflation in Singapore, the Philippines, and the Republic of Korea led to aggressive policy responses by their respective central banks (**Table 5**). The Monetary Authority of Singapore tightened during the review period, leaving the slope and width of the Singapore dollar nominal effective exchange rate unchanged, but recentering the midpoint as part of its second off-cycle adjustment since January. On 14 July, the Philippines raised its policy rate by 75 bps in an

Figure 15: Benchmark Yield Curves—Local Currency Government Bonds

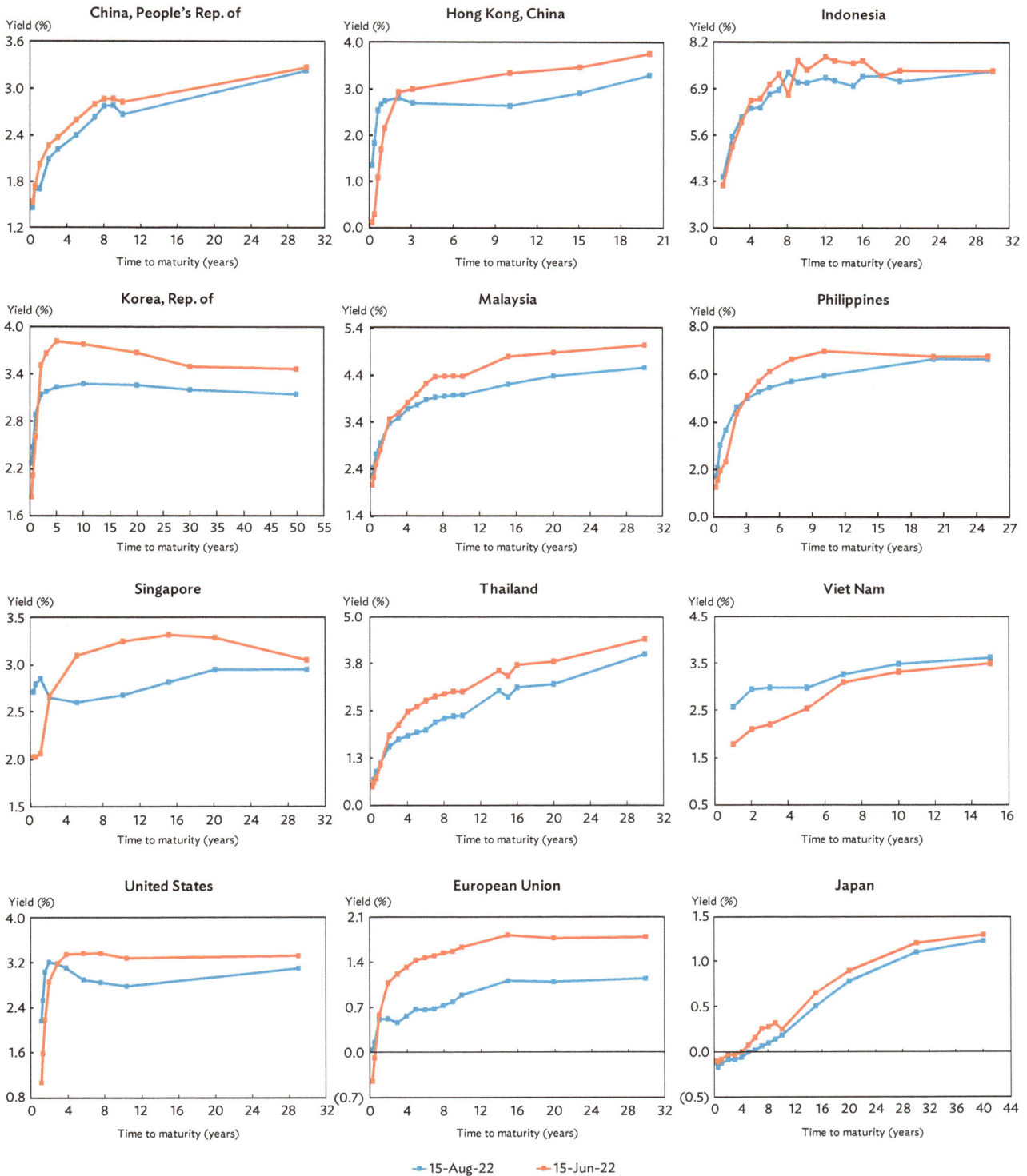

China, People's Rep. of

Hong Kong, China

Indonesia

Korea, Rep. of

Malaysia

Philippines

Singapore

Thailand

Viet Nam

United States

European Union

Japan

← 15-Aug-22   ← 15-Jun-22

( ) = negative.
Sources: Based on data from Bloomberg LP and Thai Bond Market Association.

Figure 16: Yield Spreads between 10-Year and 2-Year Government Bonds

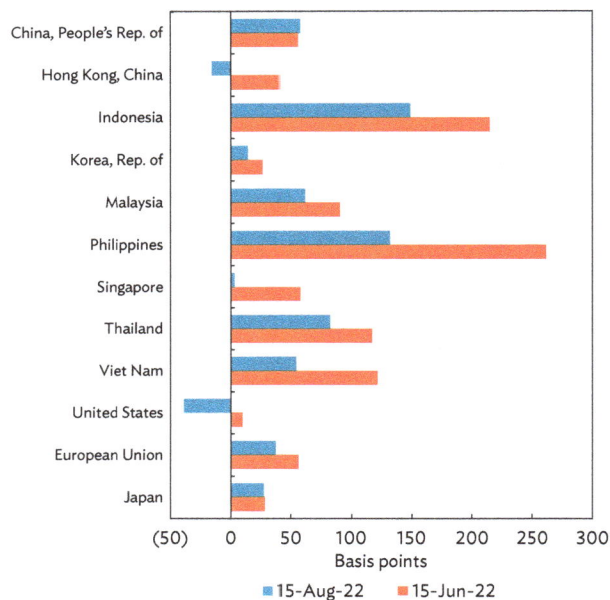

Source: *AsianBondsOnline* computations based on Bloomberg LP data.

off-cycle meeting. Previous rate hikes had been only 25 bps each in April and May. The Bangko Sentral ng Pilipinas later on raised its policy rate by 50 bps on 18 August. Likewise, the Bank of Korea raised its policy rate by 50 bps on 13 July, which exceeded previous rate hikes of 25 bps each. Subsequently, it announced another 25 bps rate hike on 25 August. Malaysia's (July) and Thailand's (August) central banks also raised their respective policy rates by 25 bps each. More recently, Bank Indonesia raised its policy rate by 25 bps on 23 August, the first time this year it has done so. Previously, Bank Indonesia opted to use other monetary tools to manage liquidity and contain inflation by raising the reserve requirement ratio, lifting 2-week to 1-year money market rates, and beginning to unwind holdings of government bonds accumulated through its burden-sharing agreement with the government. While Viet Nam has yet to adjust its policy rates, the State Bank of Vietnam has utilized open market operations to raise interest rates, using central bank bills and reverse repos to mop up liquidity.

Figure 17a: Headline Inflation Rates

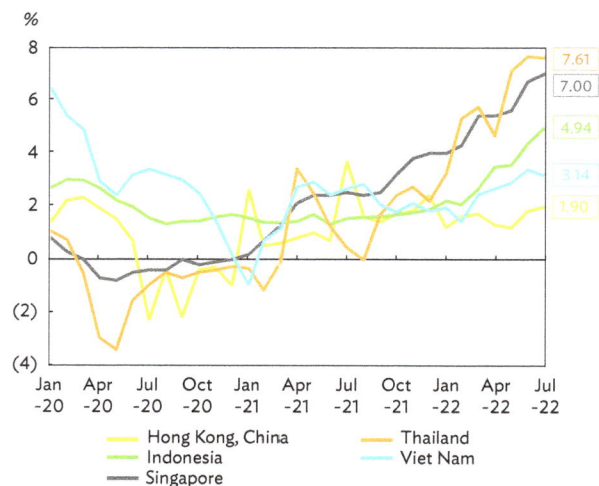

Note: Data coverage is from January 2020 to July 2022.
Source: Based on data from Bloomberg LP.

Figure 17b: Headline Inflation Rates

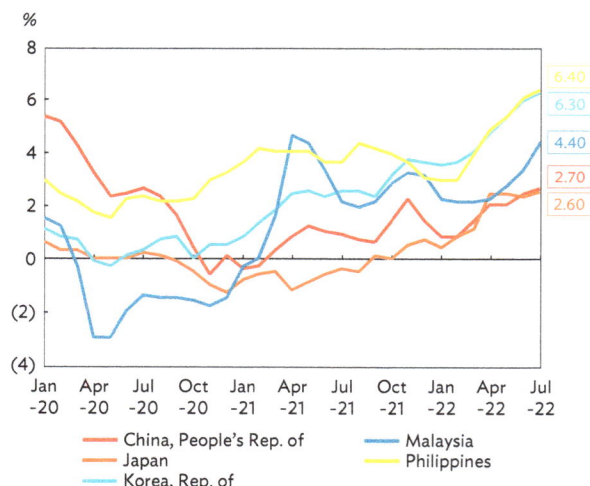

Note: Data coverage is from January 2020 to July 2022.
Source: Based on data from Bloomberg LP.

Table 5: Changes in Monetary Stances in Major Advanced Economies and Emerging East Asia

Economy	Policy Rate 15-Aug-2021 (%)	Rate Change (%)													Policy Rate 25-Aug-2022 (%)	Change in Policy Rates (basis points)
		Aug-2021	Sep-2021	Oct-2021	Nov-2021	Dec-2021	Jan-2022	Feb-2022	Mar-2022	Apr-2022	May-2022	Jun-2022	Jul-2022	Aug-2022		
United States	0.25								↑0.25		↑0.50	↑0.75	↑0.75		2.50	↑225
Euro Area	(0.50)												↑0.50		0.00	↑50
United Kingdom	0.10					↑0.15		↑0.25	↑0.25		↑0.25	↑0.25		↑0.50	1.75	↑165
Japan	(0.10)														(0.10)	
China, People's Rep. of	2.95						↓0.10							↓0.10	2.75	↓20
Indonesia	3.50													↑0.25	3.75	↑25
Korea, Rep. of	0.50	↑0.25			↑0.25		↑0.25			↑0.25	↑0.25		↑0.50	↑0.25	2.50	↑200
Malaysia	1.75										↑0.25		↑0.25		2.25	↑50
Philippines	2.00										↑0.25	↑0.25	↑0.75	↑0.50	3.75	↑175
Singapore	–		↑			↑				↑			↑		–	–
Thailand	0.50													↑0.25	0.75	↑25
Viet Nam	4.00														4.00	

( ) = negative.

Notes:
1. Data coverage is from 15 August 2021 to 25 August 2022.
2. For the People's Republic of China, data used in the chart are for the 1-year medium-term lending facility rate. While the 1-year benchmark lending rate is the official policy rate of the People's Bank of China, market players use the 1-year medium-term lending facility rate as a guide for the monetary policy direction of the People's Bank of China.
3. The up (down) arrow for Singapore signifies monetary policy tightening (loosening) by its central bank. Monetary Authority of Singapore utilizes the exchange rate to guide its monetary policy.

Sources: Various central bank websites.

Across the region, only the People's Bank of China engaged in monetary easing in recent months, as the domestic economy continued to weaken. On 15 August, the central bank reduced by 10 bps its 7-day reverse repurchase rate and the 1-year medium-term lending facility rate as part of efforts to revive economic growth. Later, on 22 August, the People's Bank of China reduced the 1-year loan prime rate by 5 bps and the 5-year loan prime rate by 15 bps.

Corporate spreads between AAA-rated and government yields largely rose.

The spread between AAA-rated yields and government yields rose during the review period in all four markets for which data are available on a softening outlook for the global economy (**Figure 18a**). These developments also led to a jump in lower-rated yields in the PRC and Malaysia (**Figure 18b**). Lower-rated yield spreads, however, were unchanged for the Republic of Korea but fell in Thailand.

Figure 18a: Credit Spreads—Local Currency Corporates Rated AAA versus Government Bonds

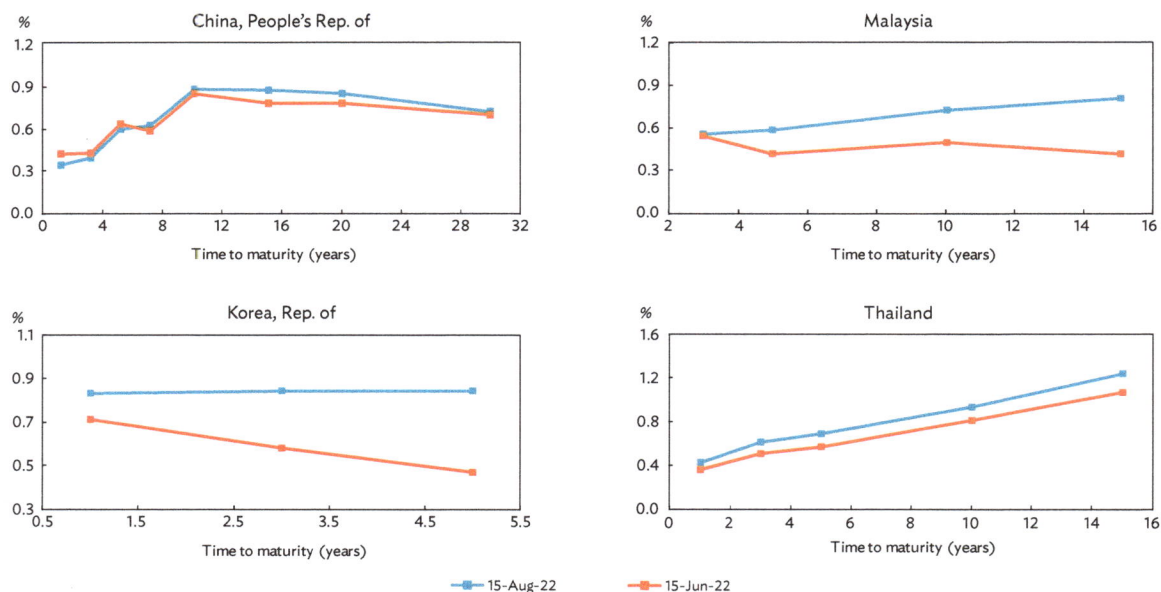

Notes:
1. Credit spreads are obtained by subtracting government yields from corporate indicative yields.
2. Corporate yields for Malaysia are as of 14 June 2022 and 12 August 2022. For the Republic of Korea, corporate yields are as of 15 June 2022 and 11 August 2022.
Sources: People's Republic of China (Bloomberg LP), Republic of Korea (KG Zeroin Corporation), Malaysia (Fully Automated System for Issuing/Tendering Bank Negara Malaysia), and Thailand (Bloomberg LP).

Figure 18b: Credit Spreads—Lower-Rated Local Currency Corporates versus AAA

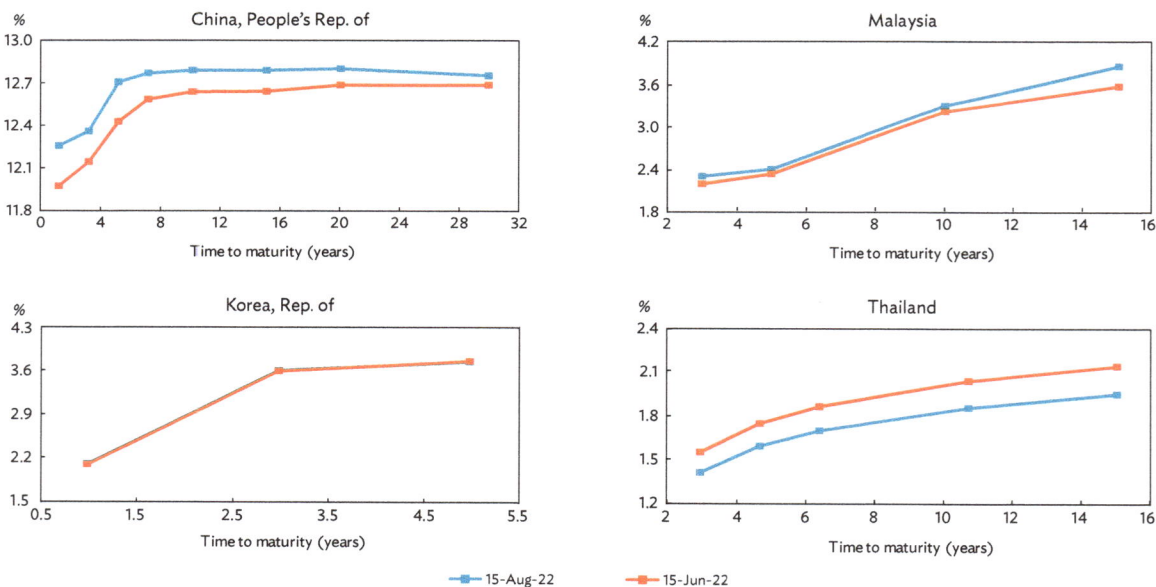

Notes:
1. Credit spreads are obtained by subtracting government yields from corporate indicative yields.
2. Corporate yields for Malaysia are as of 14 June 2022 and 12 August 2022. For the Republic of Korea, corporate yields are as of 15 June 2022 and 11 August 2022.
Sources: People's Republic of China (Bloomberg LP), Republic of Korea (KG Zeroin Corporation), Malaysia (Fully Automated System for Issuing/Tendering Bank Negara Malaysia), and Thailand (Bloomberg LP).

Recent Developments in ASEAN+3 Sustainable Bond Markets

The expansion of ASEAN+3's sustainable bond market moderated in Q2 2022.[6] By the end of June, the outstanding amount of sustainable bonds in ASEAN+3 reached USD503.5 billion on growth of 35.9% year-on-year (y-o-y) in the second (Q2) of 2022, compared to 53.1% y-o-y in the first quarter (Q1).[7] Meanwhile, quarter-on-quarter (q-o-q) growth moderated to 4.0% in Q2 2022 from 10.8% in Q1 2022 (**Figure 19**). The slowdown in growth was largely due to increased headwinds to the economic outlook and tightening financial conditions both globally and in the region. Meanwhile, the global sustainable bond market reached a size of USD3.3 trillion at the end of June, posting growth of 40.9% y-o-y and 13.4% q-o-q in Q2 2022. With higher growth rates for the global sustainable bond market than those for ASEAN+3 during the quarter, ASEAN+3's share of the total global market declined from 16.7% at the end of March to 15.3% at the end of June. Although ASEAN+3 remains the second-largest regional sustainable bond market (excluding international organizations) after Europe, the gap with Europe in terms of bonds outstanding widened from USD894.5 billion at the end of March to USD1,095.1 billion at the end of June.

Issuance in ASEAN+3's sustainable bond market declined in Q2 2022, primarily on falling issuance in the People's Republic of China and Japan. Amid dimming growth prospects and accelerated monetary tightening, aggregate sustainable bond issuance in ASEAN+3 markets declined to USD61.0 billion in Q2 2022 from USD64.4 billion in Q1 2022, posting contractions of 3.4% y-o-y and 5.2% q-o-q (**Figure 20**). The slowdown in regional issuance was largely driven by reduced issuance in the People's Republic of China (PRC) and Japan in Q2 2022, where issuance dropped to USD34.8 billion and USD9.1 billion, respectively, from USD37.7 billion and USD11.6 billion in Q1 2022. Their respective shares of the region's total issuance also fell to 57.1% and 15.0% in Q2 2022 from 58.5% and 18.1% in Q1 2022. Meanwhile, ASEAN+3's share of global sustainable bond issuance slightly declined to 24.5% in Q2 2022 from 24.7% in Q1 2022.

ASEAN is an active player in the regional sustainability and sustainability-linked bond markets. ASEAN member economies accounted for 7.5% of ASEAN+3's sustainable bond market with USD37.7 billion worth of outstanding bonds at the end of June. Despite the headwinds, ASEAN markets' issuance increased to USD4.2 billion during Q2 2022 from USD4.0 billion during Q1 2022, pushing up their aggregate share of the region's total issuance to 6.9% from 6.2% in Q1 2022. Moreover, in terms of bonds outstanding, ASEAN markets

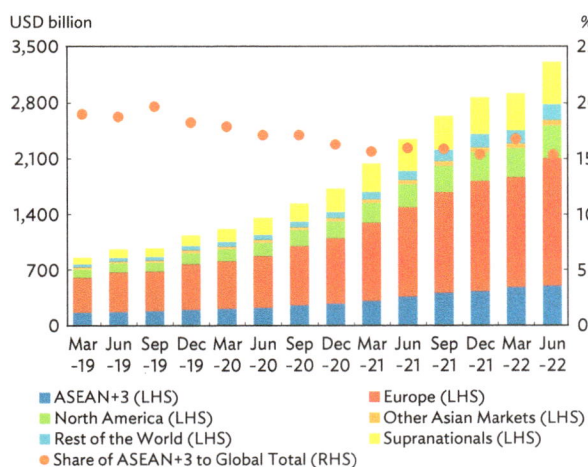

Figure 19: Sustainable Bonds Outstanding in Global Markets

USD billion / %

ASEAN = Association of Southeast Asian Nations, LHS = left-hand side, RHS = right-hand side, USD = United States dollar.
Notes:
1. ASEAN+3 includes ASEAN members Indonesia, Malaysia, the Philippines, Singapore, Thailand, and Viet Nam plus the People's Republic of China; Hong Kong, China; Japan; and the Republic of Korea.
2. Data include both local currency and foreign currency issues.
Source: *AsianBondsOnline* computations based on Bloomberg LP data.

---

[6] For the discussion on sustainable bonds, ASEAN+3 includes Association of Southeast Asian Nations (ASEAN) members Indonesia, Malaysia, the Philippines, Singapore, Thailand, and Viet Nam plus the People's Republic of China; Hong Kong, China; Japan; and the Republic of Korea.
[7] Sustainable bonds include green, social, sustainability, sustainability-linked, and transition bonds.

Figure 20: Sustainable Bond Issuance in ASEAN+3 by Market

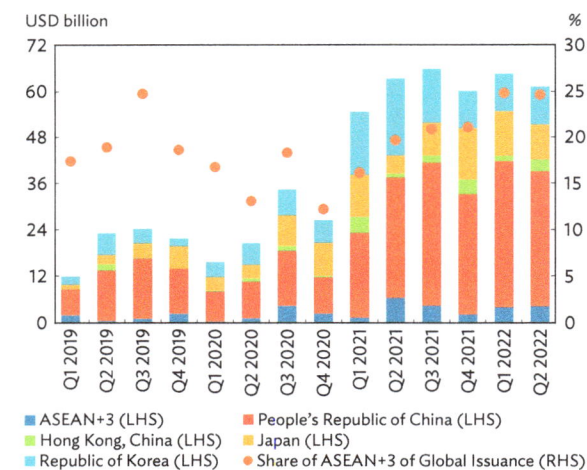

ASEAN = Association of Southeast Asian Nations; LHS = left-hand side;
Q = quarter; RHS = right-hand side; USD = United States dollar.
Notes:
1. ASEAN+3 includes ASEAN members Indonesia, Malaysia, the Philippines,
   Singapore, Thailand, and Viet Nam plus the People's Republic of China;
   Hong Kong, China; Japan; and the Republic of Korea.
2. Data include both foreign currency and local currency issues.
Source: *AsianBondsOnline* computations based on Bloomberg LP data.

Figure 21: Sustainable Bonds Outstanding in ASEAN+3 by Bond Type and Economy Share

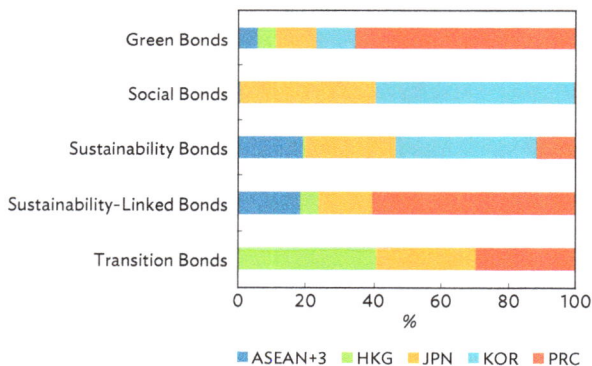

ASEAN = Association of Southeast Asian Nations; HKG = Hong Kong, China;
JPN = Japan; KOR = Republic of Korea; PRC = People's Republic of China.
Notes:
1. ASEAN+3 includes ASEAN members Indonesia, Malaysia, the Philippines,
   Singapore, Thailand, and Viet Nam plus the People's Republic of China;
   Hong Kong, China; Japan; and the Republic of Korea.
2. Data as of 30 June 2022 and include both foreign currency and local currency
   issues.
Source: *AsianBondsOnline* computations based on Bloomberg LP data.

have a significant presence in the regional sustainability bond market (19.2% of the ASEAN+3 total) and the sustainability-linked bond market (18.5% of the ASEAN+3 total). In terms of issuance, ASEAN accounted for 16.7% and 23.2%, respectively, of the region's sustainability and sustainability-linked bond issuance totals during Q2 2022. This represents a larger presence than its 12.0% share of ASEAN+3's total outstanding bonds at the end of June and 11.0% of total bond issuance during Q2 2022. Meanwhile, the PRC had the most sustainable bonds outstanding among all economies in ASEAN+3, accounting for 49.4% of the regional sustainable bond market at the end of June, though this was less than the PRC's 55.3% share of all ASEAN+3 bonds outstanding. Bonds outstanding from PRC issuers comprised a significant share of the regional green bond market (65.3%) and sustainability-linked bond market (60.2%) at the end of June (**Figure 21**). Outstanding bonds in the Republic of Korea (21.0%) and Japan (17.7%) comprised the next largest shares of the sustainable bond market and jointly accounted for nearly the entire regional social bond market at the end of June. As transition bonds are still at the very early development stage, only a few of the region's more advanced bond markets—the PRC; Hong Kong, China; and Japan—have shown activity in this market segment.

Diversification has improved in ASEAN+3 sustainable bond markets. The regional sustainable bond market has become less concentrated in recent quarters as evidenced by a decline in the Herfindahl–Hirschman Index, a common measure of market concentration (**Figure 22**). Green bonds continued to largely dominate ASEAN+3 sustainable bond markets. Outstanding green bonds increased to USD350.7 billion at the end of June, accounting for 69.7% of the region's sustainable bonds outstanding. However, the green bond share has declined in recent years as other types of sustainable bonds, especially sustainability-linked and transition bonds, continue to expand. The issuance of green and sustainability bonds declined in Q2 2022 to USD45.5 billion and USD5.4 billion, respectively, from USD50.0 billion and USD8.9 billion in Q1 2022. Meanwhile, on a q-o-q basis, issuance rose substantially for sustainability-linked bonds (175.1%), transition bonds (424.0%, albeit coming from a low base), and social bonds (37.5%) (**Figure 23**).

Figure 22: ASEAN+3 Sustainable Bonds Outstanding by Bond Type

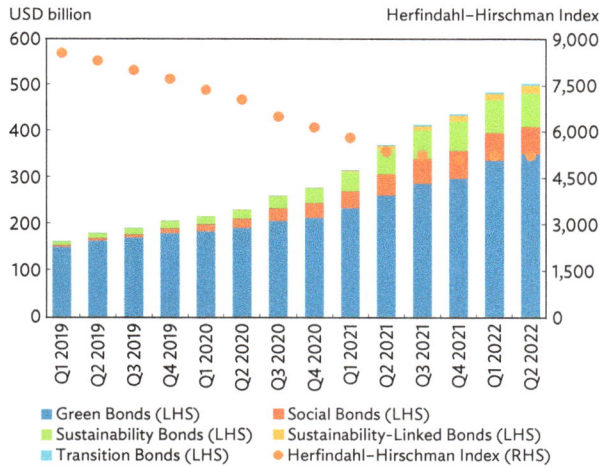

ASEAN = Association of Southeast Asian Nations, USD = United States dollar.
Notes:
1. ASEAN+3 includes ASEAN members Indonesia, Malaysia, the Philippines, Singapore, Thailand, and Viet Nam plus the People's Republic of China; Hong Kong, China; Japan; and the Republic of Korea.
2. Data include both foreign currency and local currency issues.
3. The Herfindahl–Hirschman Index is a commonly accepted measure of market concentration and is calculated by summing the squared market share of each bond type competing in the market.
Source: *AsianBondsOnline* computations based on Bloomberg LP data.

Figure 23: Sustainable Bond Issuance in ASEAN+3 by Bond Type

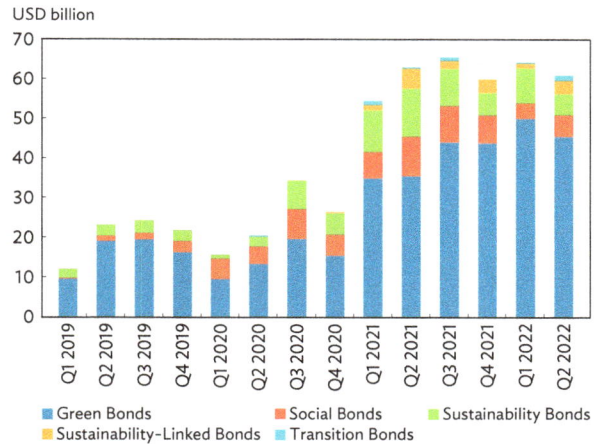

ASEAN = Association of Southeast Asian Nations, USD = United States dollar.
Notes:
1. ASEAN+3 includes ASEAN members Indonesia, Malaysia, the Philippines, Singapore, Thailand, and Viet Nam plus the People's Republic of China; Hong Kong, China; Japan; and the Republic of Korea.
2. Data include both foreign currency and local currency issues.
Source: *AsianBondsOnline* computations based on Bloomberg LP data.

The private sector dominates issuance in ASEAN+3 sustainable bond markets. The private sector accounted for 89.0% of total regional sustainable bond issuance in Q2 2022 (**Figure 24**), with financial institutions accounting for the single-largest share of private sector issuance at 45.1%. The most diversified issuer profiles during Q2 2022 were in the green and sustainability-linked bond markets. The public sector's share of total ASEAN+3 sustainable bond issuance rose to 11.0% in Q2 2022 from 9.8% in Q1 2022, with public sector issuance mainly in the form of green bonds and sustainability bonds as regional governments sought to meet their climate commitments. Specifically, governments in Indonesia and Hong Kong, China issued green bonds in Q2 2022, while the Government of the Philippines issued sustainability bonds.

Short-term, local-currency-denominated financing comprises the majority of the ASEAN+3 sustainable bond market. Outstanding sustainable bonds in ASEAN+3 remained largely concentrated in shorter tenors in Q2 2022; the average size-weighted tenor

Figure 24: Sustainable Bond Issuance in ASEAN+3 by Sector

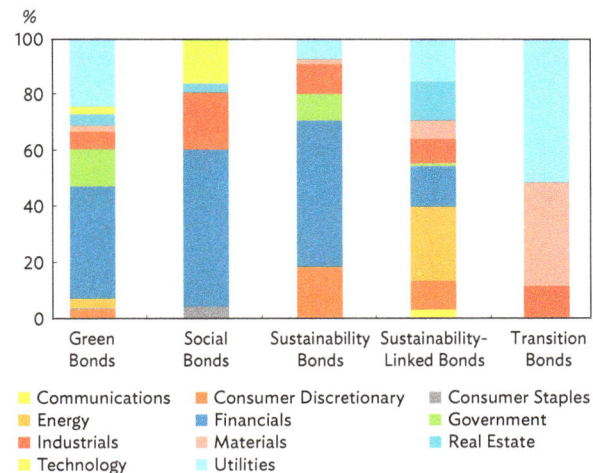

ASEAN = Association of Southeast Asian Nations.
Notes:
1. ASEAN+3 includes ASEAN members Indonesia, Malaysia, the Philippines, Singapore, Thailand, and Viet Nam plus the People's Republic of China; Hong Kong, China; Japan; and the Republic of Korea.
2. Data reflect issuance for the period 1 April 2022 to 30 June 2022 and include both foreign currency and local currency issues.
Source: *AsianBondsOnline* computations based on Bloomberg LP data.

of outstanding sustainable bonds at the end of June was 4.3 years. At the same time, 72.7% of outstanding sustainable bonds carried maturities of 5 years or less, while 61.1% of outstanding sustainable bonds in ASEAN+3 were denominated in local currencies (**Figure 25**). The use of local currency was most pronounced in the social (81.8%), sustainability-linked (79.1%), and green (61.1%) bond markets. The average size-weighted tenor of sustainable bonds issued in ASEAN+3 during Q2 2022 was 4.6 years, with green bonds having the shortest average maturity at 3.7 years. During the quarter, 67.9% of regional sustainable bond issuance was denominated in local currency—with transition, sustainability-linked, and social bonds having the highest shares of local-currency-denominated issuance (**Figure 26**).

Figure 25: Maturity and Currency Profiles of ASEAN+3 Sustainable Bonds Outstanding at the End of June 2022

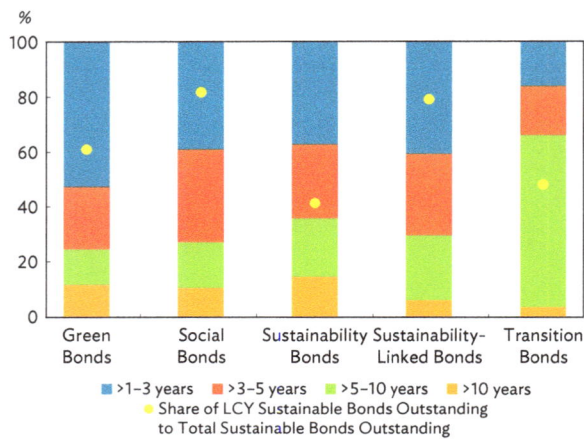

ASEAN = Association of Southeast Asian Nations, LCY = local currency.
Notes:
1. ASEAN+3 includes ASEAN members Indonesia, Malaysia, the Philippines, Singapore, Thailand, and Viet Nam plus the People's Republic of China; Hong Kong, China; Japan; and the Republic of Korea.
2. Data include both foreign currency and local currency issues
Source: *AsianBondsOnline* computations based on Bloomberg LP data.

Figure 26: Maturity and Currency Profiles of ASEAN+3 Sustainable Bond Issuance in the Second Quarter of 2022

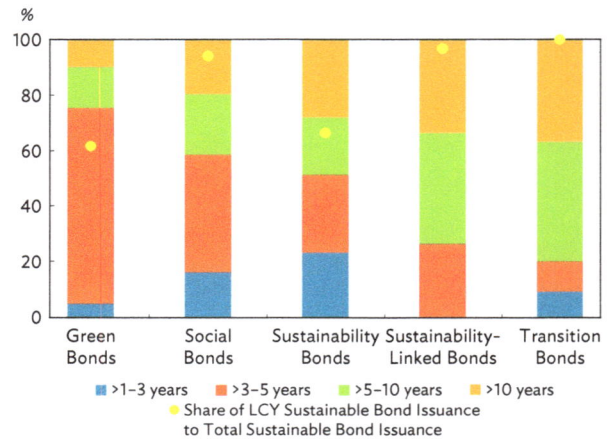

ASEAN = Association of Southeast Asian Nations, LCY = local currency.
Notes:
1. ASEAN+3 includes ASEAN members Indonesia, Malaysia, the Philippines, Singapore, Thailand, and Viet Nam plus the People's Republic of China; Hong Kong, China; Japan; and the Republic of Korea.
2. Data include both foreign currency and local currency issues.
Source: *AsianBondsOnline* computations based on Bloomberg LP data.

Policy and Regulatory Developments

People's Republic of China

The Government Unveiled 33 Stimulus Measures to Spur the Domestic Economy

In May, the Government of the People's Republic of China announced a package of 33 stimulus measures meant to shore up the domestic economy and provide support to companies in the wake of quarantine measures meant to contain the coronavirus disease (COVID-19). The measures include an expansion of companies covered by a value-added tax rebate, deferral of payments of social security premiums, an expansion of tax relief measures, a deferral of contributions to the housing provident fund, and boosted infrastructure spending, among others.

Hong Kong, China

Hong Kong Monetary Authority Participates in the Bank for International Settlements Renminbi Liquidity Arrangement

On 25 June, the Bank for International Settlements (BIS) announced a Renminbi Liquidity Arrangement developed with the People's Bank of China to provide liquidity to central banks through a new reserve pooling system. The Hong Kong Monetary Authority is among the initial group of central bank participants, which includes the People's Bank of China, Bank Indonesia, the Bank Negara Malaysia (BNM), the Monetary Authority of Singapore, and the Banco Central de Chile. To set up the reserve pool placed with the BIS, each participating central bank contributed a minimum of CNY15.0 billion. The arrangement complements existing BIS liquidity facilities in providing liquidity access to contributing central banks in times of market volatility.

Indonesia

State Budget 2023 Aims to Return Budget Deficit to Below 3.0% of Gross Domestic Product

In August, the President of Indonesia announced the government's commitment to reduce the budget deficit to within the legal cap of 3.0% of gross domestic product in 2023. The government's proposed 2023 state budget sets state revenues at IDR2,443.6 trillion and state expenditures at IDR3,041.7 trillion. Debt financing is projected to decline to IDR696.3 trillion. The 2023 state budget is guided by the following macroeconomic assumptions: (i) economic growth of 5.3%, (ii) inflation of 3.3%, and (iii) an exchange rate of IDR14,750 per USD1.0.

Republic of Korea

The Government Announces Plans to Improve Fiscal Soundness and Manage Global Economic Challenges

On 28 July, the Bank of Korea, Financial Services Commission, and Financial Supervisory Service held an emergency meeting to discuss the impact of the United States Federal Open Market Committee's July meeting on the domestic financial market. Representatives from these institutions stated that the Republic of Korea's strong fundamentals and responses to the challenges had more impact on capital flows than the interest rate reversal between United States Treasuries and domestic bonds, citing that Korean securities continued to register net foreign inflows in July. They also stated that the Republic of Korea is equipped to respond to these challenges, highlighting its high sovereign credit ratings and large foreign reserves. Nevertheless, the institutions will continue to monitor and increase the Republic of Korea's fiscal soundness and prepare preemptive measures and reforms to manage global economic challenges. These include, among others, (i) implementation of measures such as the government's emergency buyback of Korea Treasury Bonds (KTBs) and the Bank of Korea's buyback of KTBs in case of excessive volatility in the market; (ii) improvement of foreign investors' accessibility to domestic financial markets; and (iii) efforts for the Republic of Korea to join the FTSE World Government Bond Index via the introduction of a new tax scheme that will exempt income and corporate income tax on capital gains earned from nonresidents' and foreign corporations' investment in KTBs and central bank bonds.

Malaysia

Cagamas Conducts Maiden Issuance Based on Malaysia Overnight Rate

On 5 July, Cagamas, the national mortgage corporation of Malaysia issued the first floating-rate note referencing the Malaysia Overnight Rate (MYOR). Launched by the BNM in September 2021, MYOR is Malaysia's alternative reference rate to replace the London Interbank Offered Rate. MYOR is also transaction-based, allowing for a more robust reference rate and one that is reflective of active and liquid markets in Malaysia. To improve financial benchmarking in Malaysia, in March the BNM also launched the Malaysia Islamic Overnight Rate for Shariah-compliant financial products. Proceeds from Cagamas' floating-rate conventional medium-term note will be used to finance the purchase of housing loans from Malaysia's financial system.

Philippines

Bureau of the Treasury Releases Its July–August Borrowing Plan

The Bureau of the Treasury released its borrowing plan for July and August. The government planned to borrow PHP200 billion for the month of July, comprising PHP60 billion worth of Treasury bills and PHP140 billion worth of Treasury bonds with tenors ranging between 7 years and 14 years. For the month of August, the borrowing target was set at PHP215 billion: PHP75 billion in Treasury bills and PHP140 billion in Treasury bonds with tenors ranging from 3.5 years to 10 years.

Singapore

Singapore Green Bond Framework Launched

On 9 June, the Government of Singapore published its Singapore Green Bond Framework, which provides guidelines for issuances of sovereign green bonds under the government's Significant Infrastructure Government Loan Act. The framework adheres to international best practices, outlining recognized market standards, strict oversight of the selection of projects and allocation of proceeds, and evaluation of green projects. The framework also stipulates that proceeds from green bonds issued by government agencies will be used to finance green projects under the Singapore Green Plan 2030, which facilitates the economy's transition to a low-carbon economy and advances the United Nation's Sustainable Development Goals.

Thailand

Public Debt Management Office Announces Results of Bond-Switching Transactions

On 13 May, the Public Debt Management Office announced the results of bond-switching transactions for government bonds totaling THB90.0 billion. The bond swap allowed bond holders to switch bonds with shorter maturities for those with longer maturities. The bond swap involved five source bonds with remaining maturities ranging from 0.6 year to 2.6 years and 10 destination bonds with remaining maturities ranging from 4.6 years to 50.1 years. Bond swap operations provide bond holders with an opportunity to adjust their investment portfolio and allow the government to extend its debt maturity profile, thereby reducing debt redemption pressures and boosting liquidity.

Viet Nam

State Bank of Vietnam Releases Guidance for Corporates Issuing International Bonds

In July, the State Bank of Vietnam released Circular No. 10/2022/TT-NHNN to provide guidance on foreign exchange management for corporates who issue bonds without a government guarantee in the international market. The circular provides the legal framework for borrowing and paying debt issued by corporates without guarantees. It also removed the requirement for a review of the bond issuance by a state-owned commercial bank. With the streamlined procedures, the regulation will encourage corporates to tap financing for their business operations through the issuance of international bonds.

Market Summaries

People's Republic of China

Yield Movements

Between 15 June and 15 August, local currency (LCY) government bond yields in the People's Republic of China (PRC) fell for all tenors (**Figure 1**). Bond yields fell the most for the 1-year through 7-year tenors, declining an average of 20 basis points (bps), and for the 10-year tenor, which fell 16 bps. The remaining tenors fell 2–9 bps. The spread of the 10-year over 2-year tenor rose slightly by 2 bps between 15 June and 15 August.

The PRC was the sole market in the region whose entire yield curve declined, driven by economic weakness in the domestic economy. The PRC's gross domestic product barely changed in the second quarter (Q2) of 2022, gaining only 0.4% year-on-year (y-o-y) after a 4.8% y-o-y expansion in the first quarter (Q1) of 2022. Among the major sectors, only primary industry had any appreciable growth, gaining 4.4% y-o-y. In contrast, output in secondary industry grew only 0.9% y-o-y, while tertiary industry contracted 0.4% y-o-y. The weak economic growth for Q2 2022 was driven by coronavirus disease (COVID-19) control measures instituted in several cities and the resulting supply chain disruptions. In the city of Shanghai, COVID-19 quarantine protocols were eased starting 1 June.

Some economic measures improved during the review period but remained weak. Industrial production growth rates improved to 3.8% y-o-y in July and 3.9% y-o-y in June, after COVID-19 restrictions were eased, versus 0.7% y-o-y in May. However, fixed-asset investment continued to decline, with the January–July growth rate falling to 5.7% y-o-y from the January–June rate of 6.1% y-o-y. The growth rate has been continuously declining since the start of the year. Retail sales growth also moderated to 2.7% y-o-y in July after rising 3.1% y-o-y in June. The economic outlook for the PRC continued to remain negative. In July, the government announced that it was unlikely to meet its 5.5% growth target for the year. In addition, in August,

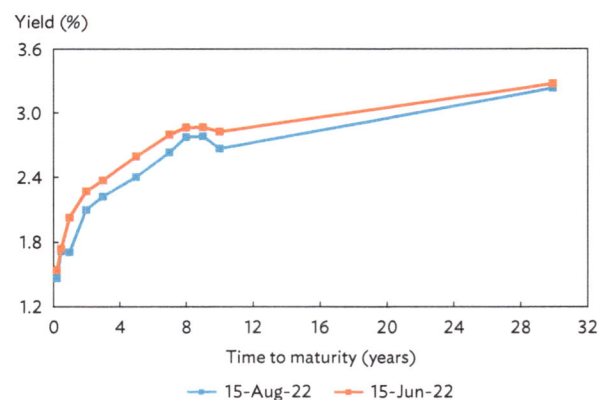

Figure 1: The People's Republic of China's Benchmark Yield Curve—Local Currency Government Bonds

Source: Based on data from Bloomberg LP.

some government officials announced that the 5.5% growth target would now serve more as guidance, with no penalties assessed should the target be missed. Consumer price inflation also continued to be muted in the PRC.

The softening outlook pushed the government to enact a slew of fiscal measures that were announced on 31 May. The measures provide support for industries such as value-added tax rebates, tax reductions for qualified industries, and a deferral on the payment of social security premiums. On 15 August, the central bank reduced by 10 bps its 7-day reverse repurchase rate to 2.10% and the 1-year medium-term lending facility to 2.75%. A week after, on 22 August, the People's Bank of China reduced the 1-year loan prime rate by 5 bps to 3.65% and the 5-year loan prime rate by 15 bps to 4.30%.

Size and Composition

The LCY bond market in the PRC grew to a size of CNY123.1 trillion (USD18.4 trillion) at the end of June (**Table 1**). Overall growth slightly rose to

Table 1: Size and Composition of the Local Currency Bond Market in the People's Republic of China

| | Outstanding Amount (billion) | | | | | | Growth Rates (%) | | | |
| | Q2 2021 | | Q1 2022 | | Q2 2022 | | Q2 2021 | | Q2 2022 | |
	CNY	USD	CNY	USD	CNY	USD	q-o-q	y-o-y	q-o-q	y-o-y
Total	106,590	16,507	118,908	18,755	123,050	18,368	3.0	14.4	3.5	15.4
Government	68,384	10,591	76,404	12,051	79,710	11,898	3.3	16.2	4.3	16.6
Treasury Bonds and Other Government Bonds	21,548	3,337	23,359	3,684	24,092	3,596	2.5	21.2	3.1	11.8
Central Bank Bonds	15	2	15	2	15	2	0.0	0.0	0.0	0.0
Policy Bank Bonds	18,658	2,890	20,107	3,171	20,213	3,017	1.5	12.0	0.5	8.3
Local Government Bonds	28,163	4,362	32,922	5,193	35,390	5,283	5.2	15.4	7.5	25.7
Corporate	38,207	5,917	42,504	6,704	43,340	6,469	2.3	11.3	2.0	13.4

CNY = Chinese yuan, q-o-q = quarter-on-quarter, Q1 = first quarter, Q2 = second quarter, USD = United States dollar, y-o-y = year-on-year.
Notes:
1. Other government bonds include savings bonds and local government bonds.
2. Bloomberg LP end-of-period local currency–USD rates are used.
3. Growth rates are calculated from local currency base and do not include currency effects.
Sources: CEIC Data Company and Bloomberg LP.

3.5% quarter-on-quarter (q-o-q) in Q2 2022 from 3.3% q-o-q in Q1 2022. Growth was capped by the weak performance of the corporate bond sector. On a y-o-y basis, bond market growth inched up to 15.4% in Q2 2022 from 14.9% in Q1 2022. The PRC remained the largest LCY bond market in emerging East Asia, accounting for 80.2% of the region's aggregate bond stock at the end of June.

Government bonds. The share of government bonds as a percentage of total LCY bonds outstanding slightly increased to 64.8% at the end of June from 64.3% at the end of March. Total government bonds outstanding reached CNY79.7 trillion, following an acceleration in growth to 4.3% q-o-q in Q2 2022 from 2.7% q-o-q in Q1 2022 on increased government bond issuance. Government bond issuance growth soared to 40.9% q-o-q in Q2 2022, rebounding from Q1 2022's 4.0% decline, driven by a resurgence in local government bond issuance.

Local government bond issuance grew by a massive 86.2% q-o-q as local governments were pushed to completely utilize the granted 2022 special bond quota of CNY3.5 trillion by the end of June to help stimulate the PRC economy. In addition, the funding obtained must already be allocated for infrastructure projects or spent by August 2022. This led local government bonds outstanding to grow 7.5% q-o-q in Q2 2022, the highest growth rate among all government bond types.

Treasury and other government bonds grew a respectable 3.1% q-o-q to CNY24.1 trillion at the end of Q2 2022,

driven by 16.3% q-o-q growth in Treasury bond issuance. Policy bank bonds only grew 0.5% q-o-q to CNY20.2 trillion; they were issued only to maintain existing bond stocks, with issuance growing 5.2% q-o-q.

Corporate bonds. The PRC's corporate bond market's performance was lackluster in Q2 2022, with growth slowing to 2.0% q-o-q from 4.2% q-o-q in Q1 2022. The negative outlook for the PRC economy and continuously declining funding rates made corporates more cautious to issue in Q2 2022. Corporate bonds outstanding reached CNY43.3 trillion at the end of June, comprising roughly 76.6% of emerging East Asia's corporate bond market.

Among the different categories of corporate bonds, listed corporate bonds accounted for the largest share, reaching CNY12.3 trillion at the end of June on growth of 1.7% q-o-q and 11.8% y-o-y (**Table 2**). However, the fastest growth came from financial bonds, which were the second-largest corporate bond type, growing 4.2% q-o-q to CNY9.7 trillion. Medium-term notes were the second-fastest-growing segment, rising 3.4% q-o-q. Outstanding commercial paper (–1.6%) and asset-back securities (–1.2%) posted q-o-q declines in Q2 2022.

The negative domestic economic environment extended corporates hesitancy to issue bonds, with issuance falling 8.8% q-o-q in Q2 2022 after falling 11.0% q-o-q in Q1 2022. Some major corporate bond types experienced declining q-o-q issuance in Q2 2022, including financial bonds, listed corporate bonds, and commercial paper (**Figure 2**).

Table 2: Corporate Bonds Outstanding in Key Categories

	Amount (CNY billion)			Growth Rate (%)			
				Q2 2021		Q2 2022	
	Q2 2021	Q1 2022	Q2 2022	q-o-q	y-o-y	q-o-q	y-o-y
Financial Bonds	8,038	9,281	9,671	1.0	18.2	4.2	20.3
Enterprise Bonds	3,808	3,930	3,961	1.0	1.0	0.8	4.0
Listed Corporate Bonds	10,986	12,079	12,282	1.0	22.1	1.7	11.8
Commercial Paper	2,279	2,886	2,840	1.0	(19.3)	(1.6)	24.6
Medium-Term Notes	7,457	8,268	8,549	1.0	2.1	3.4	14.6
Asset-Backed Securities	3,075	3,441	3,400	1.0	27.8	(1.2)	10.6

( ) = negative, CNY = Chinese yuan, q-o-q = quarter-on-quarter, Q1 = first quarter, Q2 = second quarter, y-o-y = year-on-year.
Source: CEIC Data Company.

Figure 2: Corporate Bond Issuance in Key Sectors

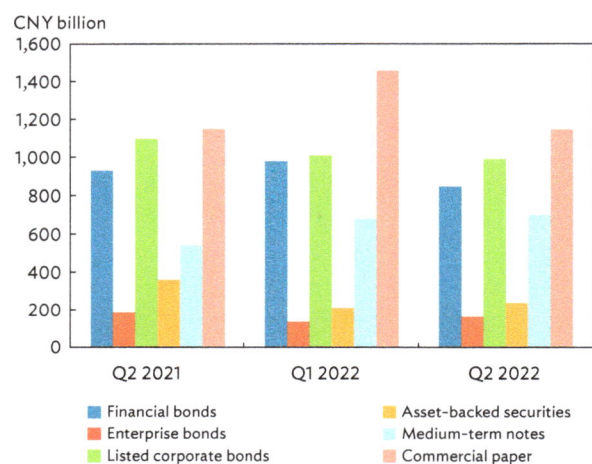

CNY = Chinese yuan, Q1 = first quarter, Q2 = second quarter.
Source: CEIC Data Company.

At the end of June, the top 30 issuers of corporate bonds in the PRC had an outstanding bond stock of CNY12.4 trillion, representing 28.7% of the corporate bond total (**Table 3**). State-owned China Railway continued to account for the largest amount of bonds outstanding at CNY3.2 trillion. Next was Bank of China with bonds outstanding of CNY888.1 billion and a 2.0% share of the corporate total. The top 30 list comprised 16 state-owned firms and 21 listed firms.

The largest corporate bond issuances in the PRC for Q2 2022 are listed in **Table 4**. Three banks and two state-owned institutions made up the largest issuances.

Banks continued to be major issuers of bonds as they beefed up their capital and funding for lending activities, while China State Railway issued bonds for infrastructure development. The State Grid Corporation issued largely short-term bonds during the quarter. Among the issuances in the list, the shortest-dated tenor was a 135-day bond and the longest-dated tenors were two perpetual bonds.

Investor Profile

Government bonds. At the end of June, banking institutions remained the largest investor group in the PRC's government bond market (**Figure 3**). The shares of banks' holdings for Treasury bonds, policy bank bonds, and local government bonds stood at 54.8%, 65.8%, and 86.3%, respectively, at the end of the review period. However, the respective shares for policy bank bonds and local government bonds declined compared with the same period a year earlier.

Continued outflows from the PRC bond market in Q2 2022 caused the foreign holdings share to slip as declining domestic interest rates narrowed the interest rate differential with the US, making bonds less attractive. The foreign holdings share of policy bank bonds dipped to 4.2% in Q2 2022 from 5.5% in Q2 2021. For Treasury bonds, the foreign holdings share fell to 10.7% from 11.1% over the same period. The foreign holdings share of local government bonds remained very small (0.03%). Local government bonds were largely held by commercial banks, which accounted for over 80% share.

Table 3: Top 30 Issuers of Local Currency Corporate Bonds in the People's Republic of China

	Issuers	Outstanding Amount		State-Owned	Listed Company	Type of Industry
		LCY Bonds (CNY billion)	LCY Bonds (USD billion)			
1.	China Railway	3,211.5	506.55	Yes	No	Transportation
2.	Bank of China	888.1	140.08	Yes	Yes	Banking
3.	Industrial and Commercial Bank of China	841.0	132.65	Yes	Yes	Banking
4.	Agricultural Bank of China	800.0	126.18	Yes	Yes	Banking
5.	China Construction Bank	563.0	88.80	Yes	No	Asset Management
6.	Bank of Communications	549.7	86.70	Yes	Yes	Banking
7.	Shanghai Pudong Development Bank	522.2	82.37	Yes	Yes	Banking
8.	Industrial Bank	407.6	64.29	No	Yes	Banking
9.	Central Huijin Investment	386.0	60.88	No	Yes	Banking
10.	State Grid Corporation of China	372.0	58.68	No	Yes	Power
11.	China Citic Bank	325.0	51.26	No	Yes	Banking
12.	China Minsheng Bank	295.0	46.53	Yes	No	Energy
13.	State Power Investment	260.0	41.01	Yes	No	Power
14.	China Merchants Bank	257.2	40.57	Yes	Yes	Banking
15.	Postal Savings Bank of China	240.0	37.85	Yes	Yes	Coal
16.	China Everbright Bank	221.2	34.89	No	Yes	Banking
17.	Huaxia Bank	220.0	34.70	No	Yes	Banking
18.	China National Petroleum	185.3	29.23	No	Yes	Banking
19.	China Southern Power Grid	180.5	28.47	No	Yes	Banking
20.	Ping An Bank	180.0	28.39	No	Yes	Banking
21.	Shaanxi Coal and Chemical Industry Group	175.0	27.60	No	Yes	Brokerage
22.	Tianjin Infrastructure Investment Group	167.3	26.38	Yes	Yes	Brokerage
23.	CITIC Securities	157.9	24.90	Yes	No	Public Utilities
24.	China Merchants Securities	156.7	24.71	Yes	Yes	Brokerage
25.	Bank of Beijing	155.9	24.59	No	Yes	Banking
26.	Huatai Securities	153.5	24.20	No	No	Brokerage
27.	Guotai Junan Securities	142.8	22.52	No	Yes	Brokerage
28.	Shenwan Hongyuan Securities	141.7	22.35	Yes	No	Brokerage
29.	China Chengtong Holdings	135.4	21.36	Yes	No	Holding Company
30.	China Guangfa Bank	135.0	21.29	No	No	Banking
	Total Top 30 LCY Corporate Issuers	**12,426.2**	**1,854.9**			
	Total LCY Corporate Bonds	**43,339.8**	**6,469.3**			
	Top 30 as % of Total LCY Corporate Bonds	**28.7%**	**28.7%**			

CNY = Chinese yuan, LCY = local currency, USD = United States dollar.
Notes:
1. Data as of 30 June 2022.
2. State-owned firms are defined as those in which the government has more than a 50% ownership stake.
Source: *AsianBondsOnline* calculations based on Bloomberg LP data.

Table 4: Notable Local Currency Corporate Bond Issuances in the Second Quarter of 2022

Corporate Issuers	Coupon Rate (%)	Issued Amount (CNY billion)
Bank of China[a]		
3-year bond	2.75	35
3-year bond	2.75	5
Perpetual bond	3.65	30
Perpetual bond	3.65	20
State Grid Corporation[a]		
135-day bond	2.00	5
280-day bond	2.00	14
345-day bond	2.04	5
345-day bond	2.04	2
345-day bond	2.04	2
345-day bond	2.00	9
345-day bond	2.00	3
345-day bond	2.00	9
345-day bond	2.04	9
345-day bond	2.00	10
345-day bond	2.04	9
345-day bond	2.04	3
China Construction Bank		
3-year bond	2.60	10
10-year bond	3.45	45
15-year bond	3.65	15
Industrial and Commercial Bank of China		
3-year bond	2.60	10
10-year bond	3.50	45
15-year bond	3.74	5
China State Railway Group[a]		
5-year bond	2.97	10
10-year bond	3.25	10
10-year bond	3.22	8
20-year bond	3.46	10
30-year bond	3.53	12
30-year bond	3.56	10

CNY = Chinese yuan.
[a] Multiple issuance of the same tenor indicates issuance on different dates.
Source: Based on data from Bloomberg LP.

Figure 3: Local Currency Treasury Bonds and Policy Bank Bonds Investor Profile

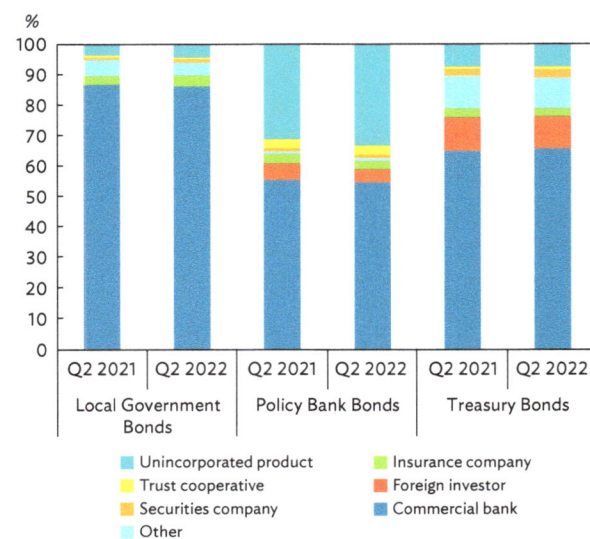

Q2 = second quarter.
Source: CEIC Data Company.

Policy, Institutional, and Regulatory Developments

The Government Unveiled 33 Stimulus Measures to Spur the Domestic Economy

In May, the Government of the PRC announced a package of 33 stimulus measures meant to shore up the domestic economy and provide support to companies in the wake of quarantine measures meant to contain COVID-19. The measures include an expansion of companies covered by a value-added tax rebate, deferral of payments of social security premiums, an expansion of tax relief measures, a deferral of contributions to the housing provident fund, and boosted infrastructure spending, among others.

Hong Kong, China

Yield Movements

Between 15 June and 15 August, Hong Kong, China's local currency (LCY) government bond yield curve inverted, as yields rose for bonds with maturities of less than 2 years but fell for bonds with longer tenors (**Figure 1**). Yields for bonds with maturities of less than 2 years climbed an average of 115 basis points (bps). In contrast, yields for bonds with maturities of 2 years and longer dropped 43 bps on average. The 2-year yield shed 13 bps, while the 10-year yield plunged 70 bps. The yield curve's inversion started at the end of July and deepened toward the end of the review period. On 15 August, the spread between the 10-year and 2-year yields remained inverted at –16 bps.

Hong Kong, China's LCY bond yield movements during the review period tracked those of United States (US) Treasury yields as the Hong Kong dollar is pegged to the US dollar.[8] Yields for shorter-term US Treasuries jumped amid accelerated rate hikes by the US Federal Reserve, while yields for longer-term government debt fell, reflecting fears that the pace of monetary policy tightening could hamper economic recovery. The US Treasury yield curve was consistently inverted from 5 July through the end of the review period, with the 2-year outpacing the 10-year Treasury yield by as much as 39 bps on 15 August.

To rein in persistent inflation, the Federal Reserve raised the target range for its policy rate by 75 bps to 1.50%–1.75% in June and by an additional 75 bps to 2.25%–2.50% in July. To maintain the Hong Kong dollar's peg to the US dollar, the Hong Kong Monetary Authority (HKMA) adjusted its base rate by 75 bps to 2.00% on 16 June and by another 75 bps to 2.75% on 28 July. The rate hikes created upward pressure on yields at the shorter-end of government bond yield curves in both the US and Hong Kong, China.

The inversion in Hong Kong, China's LCY government bond yield curve also reflected lingering weakness in the domestic economy. Hong Kong, China's gross domestic product (GDP) contracted 1.3% year-on-year (y-o-y) in the second quarter (Q2) of 2022, following a decline

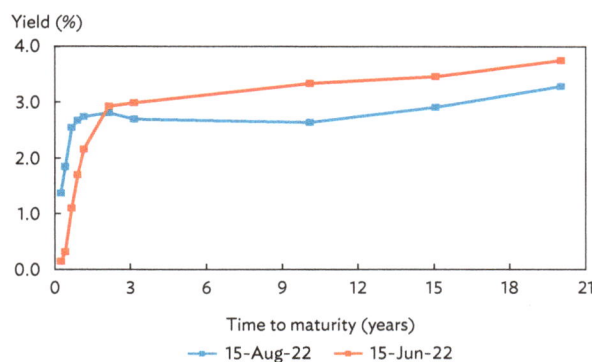

Figure 1: Hong Kong, China's Benchmark Yield Curve—Exchange Fund Bills and Notes

Source: Based on data from Bloomberg LP.

of 3.9% y-o-y in the first quarter (Q1). The contraction in merchandise exports deepened to 8.6% y-o-y in Q2 2022 from 4.5% y-o-y in Q1 2022, driven primarily by weaker exports to the People's Republic of China. Private consumption posted modest growth of 0.1% y-o-y in Q2 2022, a recovery from the 5.8% y-o-y drop in the previous quarter, as the relaxation of social distancing and government relief measures boosted demand. Government expenditure rose 13.0% y-o-y in Q2 2022, supported by spending on recovery efforts. The decline in investments narrowed to 3.0% y-o-y in Q2 2022 from 7.8% y-o-y in the prior quarter amid a slight revival of business sentiment. Given the weak performance in Q1 and Q2, and worsening global growth prospects, the government lowered its full-year 2022 GDP growth forecast in August to between –0.5% and 0.5% from a forecast of 1.0%–2.0% announced in May.

Inflation in Hong Kong, China remained moderate compared to that of other economies in the region. Consumer price inflation rose 1.9% y-o-y in July, following an increase of 1.8% y-o-y in June. The Census and Statistics Department expects inflation in the near-term to remain moderate as domestic cost pressure continues to be modest. The government's August forecast for full-year 2022 headline inflation remained at 2.1%, the same as its May projection.

---

8 The Hong Kong dollar is pegged to a narrow band of between 7.75 and 7.85 versus the US dollar. The base rate is set at either 50 bps above the lower end of the prevailing target range of the US Federal Reserve rate or the average of the 5-day moving averages of the overnight and 1-month Hong Kong Interbank Offered Rate, whichever is higher.

Size and Composition

Hong Kong, China's LCY bond market expanded 2.1% quarter-on-quarter (q-o-q) and 7.1% y-o-y in Q2 2022 to reach a size of HKD2,599.3 billion (USD331.3 billion) at the end of June (**Table 1**). Growth accelerated from 0.8% q-o-q and 4.1% y-o-y in Q1 2022, driven by a rebound in the corporate bond segment. Growth in the government bond segment dropped to near-zero in Q2 2022 from 3.3% q-o-q in the previous quarter. Meanwhile, the corporate bond segment registered a 4.4% q-o-q expansion in Q2 2022, reversing the 1.9% q-o-q decline in the preceding quarter. Robust issuance underpinned the expansion in corporate bonds. In terms of composition, Hong Kong, China's LCY bond market had a slightly higher share of government bonds (52.4%) than corporate bonds (47.6%) at the end of June.

Government bonds. Outstanding LCY government bonds totaled HKD1,361.1 billion at the end of June. Quarterly growth in Q2 2022 was marginal, as outstanding Exchange Fund Bills (EFBs) inched up 0.2% q-o-q, while outstanding Exchange Fund Notes (EFNs) and Hong Kong Special Administrative Region (HKSAR) bonds dropped 3.4% q-o-q and 0.4% q-o-q, respectively. On an annual basis, the government bond segment expanded 12.0% y-o-y in Q2 2022, down from 14.6% y-o-y in Q1 2022.

Total issuance of new government bonds reached HKD957.0 billion in Q2 2022 after rising 1.7% q-o-q and 11.9% y-o-y. Growth stemmed primarily from increased issuance of HKSAR bonds, which rose 157.6% q-o-q during the review period.

Exchange Fund Bills. EFBs outstanding totaled HKD1,167.8 billion at the end of June on growth of 0.2% q-o-q and 11.8% y-o-y. EFBs continued to be the most dominant type of government bond, comprising 85.8% of total government bonds at the end of June. EFB issuance growth eased to 1.1% q-o-q in Q2 2022 from 3.0% q-o-q in the previous quarter.

Exchange Fund Notes. Outstanding EFNs amounted to HKD22.6 billion at the end of June after contracting 3.4% q-o-q and 6.6% y-o-y in Q2 2022. Since 2015, issuance of EFNs has been limited to the 2-year tenor. The HKMA issued HKD2.0 billion of such EFNs in May with a record-high coupon of 2.35%. EFNs continued to be the least dominant type of government bond, accounting for 1.7% of the total at the end of June.

HKSAR bonds. The outstanding stock of HKSAR bonds reached HKD170.7 billion at the end of June after a decline of 0.4% q-o-q. Bonds issued under the Institutional Bond Issuance Programme totaled HKD8.5 billion in Q2 2022. This included the inaugural issuance of 20-year bonds amounting to HKD0.5 billion in May. In addition, the government issued HKD4.0 billion of 3-year bonds in April, HKD1.5 billion of 1-year floating-rate notes indexed to the Hong Kong Overnight Index Average in May, and HKD2.5 billion of 5-year bonds in June. HKSAR bonds accounted for 12.5% of total LCY government bonds outstanding at the end of June.

Table 1: Size and Composition of the Local Currency Bond Market in Hong Kong, China

| | Outstanding Amount (billion) | | | | | | Growth Rate (%) | | | |
| | Q2 2021 | | Q1 2022 | | Q2 2022 | | Q2 2021 | | Q2 2022 | |
	HKD	USD	HKD	USD	HKD	USD	q-o-q	y-o-y	q-o-q	y-o-y
Total	2,427	313	2,546	325	2,599	331	(0.8)	7.0	2.1	7.1
Government	1,216	157	1,361	174	1,361	173	2.4	5.1	0.04	12.0
Exchange Fund Bills	1,044	134	1,166	149	1,168	149	0.08	0.2	0.2	11.8
Exchange Fund Notes	24	3	23	3	23	3	(3.2)	(6.2)	(3.4)	(6.6)
HKSAR Bonds	147	19	171	22	171	22	23.6	66.4	(0.4)	15.9
Corporate	1,211	156	1,186	151	1,238	158	(3.7)	8.9	4.4	2.2

( ) = negative, HKD = Hong Kong dollar, HKSAR = Hong Kong Special Administrative Region, q-o-q = quarter-on-quarter, Q1 = first quarter, Q2 = second quarter, USD = United States dollar, y-o-y = year-on-year.
Notes:
1. Bloomberg LP end-of-period local currency–USD rates are used.
2. Growth rates are calculated from local currency base and do not include currency effects.
Source: Hong Kong Monetary Authority.

Corporate bonds. Hong Kong, China's LCY corporate bond market growth rebounded in Q2 2022 to reach a size of HKD1,238.2 billion at the end of June. The LCY corporate bond market expanded 4.4% q-o-q and 2.2% y-o-y in Q2 2022, reversing the 1.9% q-o-q and 5.8% y-o-y contractions in the previous quarter. Strong issuance supported the growth, as investor confidence improved during the review period amid the easing of movement restrictions.

The outstanding LCY bonds of the top 30 nonbank issuers in Hong Kong, China amounted to HKD317.8 billion at the end of June, accounting for 25.7% of the total LCY corporate bond market (**Table 2**). The Hong Kong Mortgage Corporation remained the largest issuer; its outstanding corporate debt of HKD87.4 billion at end of June comprised 7.1% of the total LCY corporate bond market. A distant second was Sung Hung Kai & Co. with outstanding corporate debt of HKD20.6 billion. The Hong Kong and China Gas Company, New World Development, and Henderson Land Development were the next largest issuers with outstanding bonds of HKD17.5 billion, HKD15.3 billion, and HKD14.1 billion, respectively, at the end of June. The top issuers were predominantly finance and real estate firms. Most corporate issuers were listed on the Hong Kong Stock Exchange, and only three were state-owned companies.

Corporate bond issuance during the review period amounted to HKD249.9 billion. Issuance growth almost tripled to 15.6% q-o-q in Q2 2022 from 5.5% q-o-q in the previous quarter, boosted by improved business sentiment amid the relaxation of social distancing measures.

Table 3 shows notable issuances of the top corporate issuers in Q2 2022. The Hong Kong Mortgage Corporation was the largest issuer with a total of HKD17.3 billion from 38 issuances, the longest of which was a 3-year bond with a 3.66% coupon. The state-owned Airport Authority was the next largest issuer in Q2 2022, with six issuances totaling HKD5.0 billion. Haitong International raised a total of HKD1.8 billion from short-term bonds, including the largest single issuance in Q2 2022: a 215-day bond worth HKD1.7 billion. Issuances during the review period had notably shorter maturities compared with the previous quarter. The longest tenor issued in Q2 2022 were 3-year bonds issued by The Hong Kong Mortgage Corporation, The Hong Kong and China Gas Company, and The Wharf (Holdings).

Policy, Institutional, and Regulatory Developments

Hong Kong Monetary Authority Participates in the Bank for International Settlements Renminbi Liquidity Arrangement

On 25 June, the Bank for International Settlements (BIS) announced a Renminbi Liquidity Arrangement developed with the People's Bank of China to provide liquidity to central banks through a new reserve pooling system. The HKMA is among the initial group of central bank participants, which includes the People's Bank of China, Bank Indonesia, the Bank Negara Malaysia, the Monetary Authority of Singapore, and the Banco Central de Chile. To set up the reserve pool placed with the BIS, each participating central bank contributed a minimum of CNY15.0 billion. The arrangement complements existing BIS liquidity facilities in providing liquidity access to contributing central banks in times of market volatility.

Hong Kong Monetary Authority Holds Countercyclical Capital Buffer at 1.0%

On 2 August, the HKMA decided to hold the countercyclical capital buffer (CCyB) ratio unchanged at 1.0%. The HKMA noted that although the latest data indicated a stabilization of economic activities, uncertainties from global and domestic factors remained elevated. Maintaining the CCyB at its current level and monitoring the economic situation was deemed appropriate. The CCyB is an integral part of the Basel III regulatory capital framework intended to strengthen the resilience of the banking sector globally.

Table 2: Top 30 Nonbank Corporate Issuers of Local Currency Corporate Bonds in Hong Kong, China

	Issuers	Outstanding Amount		State-Owned	Listed Company	Type of Industry
		LCY Bonds (HKD billion)	LCY Bonds (USD billion)			
1.	The Hong Kong Mortgage Corporation	87.4	11.1	Yes	No	Finance
2.	Sun Hung Kai & Co.	20.6	2.6	No	Yes	Finance
3.	The Hong Kong and China Gas Company	17.5	2.2	No	Yes	Utilities
4.	New World Development	15.3	1.9	No	Yes	Diversified
5.	Henderson Land Development	14.1	1.8	No	Yes	Real Estate
6.	Airport Authority	13.8	1.8	Yes	No	Transportation
7.	Hang Lung Properties	13.1	1.7	No	Yes	Real Estate
8.	Hongkong Land	12.0	1.5	No	No	Real Estate
9.	The Wharf (Holdings)	10.9	1.4	No	Yes	Finance
10.	CK Asset Holdings	10.0	1.3	No	Yes	Real Estate
11.	Link Holdings	9.8	1.3	No	Yes	Finance
12.	MTR	9.8	1.2	Yes	Yes	Transportation
13.	Swire Pacific	9.3	1.2	No	Yes	Diversified
14.	AIA Group	8.9	1.1	No	Yes	Insurance
15.	Cathay Pacific	8.7	1.1	No	Yes	Transportation
16.	Hongkong Electric	8.5	1.1	No	No	Utilities
17.	CLP Power Hong Kong Financing	7.4	0.9	No	No	Finance
18.	Swire Properties	7.3	0.9	No	Yes	Diversified
19.	Hysan Development Corporation	5.9	0.8	No	Yes	Real Estate
20.	Guotai Junan International Holdings	3.6	0.5	No	Yes	Finance
21.	Wheelock and Company	3.3	0.4	No	Yes	Real Estate
22.	Haitong International	3.1	0.4	No	Yes	Finance
23.	Lerthai Group	3.0	0.4	No	Yes	Real Estate
24.	Farsail Goldman International	2.4	0.3	No	No	Finance
25.	Ev Dynamics Holdings	2.4	0.3	No	Yes	Diversified
26.	South Shore Holdings	2.2	0.3	No	Yes	Industrial
27.	Future Days	2.2	0.3	No	No	Transportation
28.	IFC Development	2.0	0.3	No	No	Finance
29.	Nan Fung	1.8	0.2	No	No	Real Estate
30.	Champion REIT	1.7	0.2	No	Yes	Real Estate
Total Top 30 Nonbank LCY Corporate Issuers		**317.8**	**40.5**			
Total LCY Corporate Bonds		**1,238.2**	**157.8**			
Top 30 as % of Total LCY Corporate Bonds		**25.7%**	**25.7%**			

HKD = Hong Kong dollar, LCY = local currency, REIT = real estate investment trust, USD = United States dollar.
Notes:
1. Data as of 30 June 2022.
2. State-owned firms are defined as those in which the government has more than a 50% ownership stake.
Source: *AsianBondsOnline* calculations based on Bloomberg LP data.

Table 3: Notable Local Currency Corporate Bond Issuances in the Second Quarter of 2022

Corporate Issuers	Coupon Rate (%)	Issued Amount (HKD million)
The Hong Kong Mortgage Corporation[a]		
90-day bond	0.00	515
0.5-year bond	0.00	1,000
0.9-year bond	2.50	1,000
0.9-year bond	2.50	1,000
1-year bond	1.70	1,000
2-year bond	2.63	460
3-year bond	3.66	250
Airport Authority[a]		
2-year bond	2.80	1,500
2-year bond	2.80	1,000
2-year bond	2.80	1,000
Haitong International[a]		
0.6-year bond	2.10	1,700
0.6-year bond	2.00	100
Henderson Land[a]		
2-year bond	3.80	1,000
2-year bond	2.40	300
2-year bond	3.45	150
The Wharf (Holdings)		
2-year bond	2.85	400
3-year bond	3.40	300
The Hong Kong and China Gas Company[a]		
3-year bond	3.20	300
3-year bond	2.35	250

HKD = Hong Kong dollar.
[a] Multiple issuance of the same tenor indicates issuance on different dates.
Source: Bloomberg LP.

Indonesia

Yield Movements

Local currency (LCY) government bond yields in Indonesia edged down for most maturities from 15 June to 15 August (**Figure 1**). Bond yields declined an average of 35 basis points (bps) for all maturities of 4 years and longer except for the 8-year tenor. On the other hand, bond yields for maturities of 3 years or less rose an average of 23 bps during the review period, while the 8-year maturity gained the most at 63 bps. As the yield curve flattened, the spread between the 10-year and 2-year maturities narrowed from 215 bps on 15 June to 149 bps on 15 August.

Bond yields declined overall, influenced by improved sentiment as the market widely expected the United States (US) Federal Reserve to slow the aggressive pace of its rate hikes amid a weakening economic recovery and seemingly peaking inflation. Tracking movements in US yields, Indonesian government bond yields mostly trended down.

The decline in yields was also reflective of expectations the government would incur a narrower budget deficit in 2022 equivalent to 3.9% of gross domestic product (GDP) versus an earlier projection of 4.5% of GDP. Higher-than-expected government revenues from tax receipts, strong exports, and rising commodity prices allowed the government to reduce its planned bond issuance for the year. For the first 7 months of 2022, the government posted a budget surplus of IDR106.1 trillion, equivalent to 0.6% of GDP. The government remains committed to returning the budget deficit to the legally allowed level of 3.0% of GDP by 2023.

While Bank Indonesia has continued to maintain an accommodative monetary policy stance as core inflation remains low, it is optimizing the use of other monetary tools to manage inflation and liquidity conditions. Bank Indonesia held steady the 7-day reverse repurchase rate at 3.50% from February 2021 to July 2022. The deposit facility rate (2.75%) and lending facility rate (4.25%) were also held unchanged during the central bank's Board of Governors meeting on 20–21 July. During the Board of Governors meeting on 22-23 August, however, the central bank raised by 25 bps its policy rate to 3.75%, the first time it has done so this year.

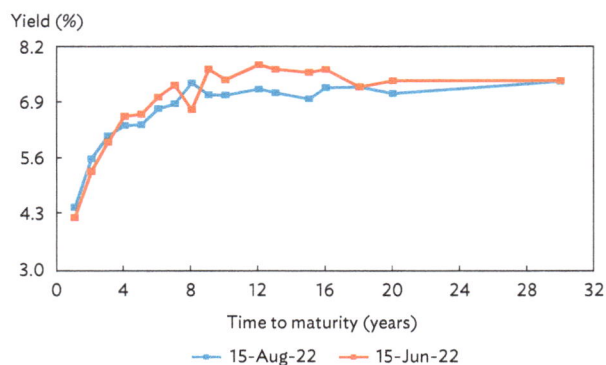

Figure 1: Indonesia's Benchmark Yield Curve— Local Currency Government Bonds

Source: Based on data from Bloomberg LP.

Yields at the shorter-end of the curve were pressured upwards by Bank Indonesia's pre-emptive and mitigating action to curb inflation by accelerating monetary policy normalization, as announced in the July Board of Governors meeting. This will be done through open market operations meant to lift rates for the 2-weeks to 1-year maturities. The central bank has also begun to offload government bonds with maturities of up to 5 years that it has accumulated under the burden-sharing agreement with the government. Also contributing to the rise in yields was the inflation spike in July to 4.9% year-on-year (y-o-y), the highest rate in 7 years, due to faster increase in food prices. In August, consumer price inflation eased to 4.7% y-o-y. Consumer price inflation has been inching up since the start of the year, albeit it is still modest compared with peers in the region.

Meanwhile, real GDP growth climbed to 5.4% y-o-y in the second quarter (Q2) of 2022 from 5.0% y-o-y in the first quarter (Q1). The improved economic performance was fueled by strong growth in household consumption, which rose to 5.5% y-o-y in Q2 2022 from 4.3% y-o-y in Q1 2022. A robust export performance also sustained the expansion, with export growth rising to 19.7% y-o-y in Q2 2022 from 16.7% y-o-y in Q1 2022. In the same period, growth in investments slowed to 3.1% y-o-y from 4.1% y-o-y, while government spending contracted by 5.2% y-o-y in Q2 2022 versus a 7.6% y-o-y decline in Q1 2022. Bank Indonesia expects GDP growth for full-year 2022 to lean toward the upper end of its forecast range of 4.5%–5.3%.

Size and Composition

Indonesia's LCY bond market grew marginally in Q2 2022 to reach a size of IDR5,497.2 trillion (USD369.0 billion) at the end of June (**Table 1**). Overall growth decelerated to 0.3% quarter-on-quarter (q-o-q) in Q2 2022 from 3.1% q-o-q in Q1 2022 due to a slowdown in issuance across all bond types. Indonesia's Q2 2022 q-o-q growth was the slowest in emerging East Asia. On a y-o-y basis, Indonesia's LCY bond market growth moderated to 11.9% in Q2 2022 from 14.1% in the preceding quarter.

Indonesia continued to account for the second-largest *sukuk* (Islamic bond) market in emerging East Asia after Malaysia. The amount of *sukuk* outstanding as a share of the total bond market remained relatively small but rose slightly to 18.2% at the end of June from 17.5% in the earlier quarter. Conventional bonds continued to account for a dominant share (81.8%) of Indonesia's LCY bond market at the end of Q2 2022.

Government bonds. The outstanding government bond stock reached IDR5,057.7 trillion at the end of June from IDR5,028.8 trillion at the end of March. Growth was marginal at 0.6% q-o-q in Q2 2022, moderating from 3.0% q-o-q in Q1 2022. On an annual basis, the government bond segment recorded slower growth of 12.7% y-o-y in Q2 2022 versus 15.2% y-o-y in Q1 2022. Government bonds continued to dominate Indonesia's

LCY bond market, accounting for a 92.0% share of the total at the end of June and representing the largest share of government bonds to total bonds in emerging East Asia.

Central government bonds and nontradable bonds. At the end of June, the outstanding stock of central government bonds, which comprised tradable Treasury bills and bonds, rose a marginal 0.4% q-o-q in Q2 2022 compared with 7.4% q-o-q in Q1 2022. The slower growth stemmed from volumes of issuance and maturities being broadly at par during the quarter. On a y-o-y basis, growth in the central government bond stock eased to 13.2% in Q2 2022 from 16.2% in Q1 2022. In the same period, nontradable bonds outstanding climbed to IDR144.4 trillion on growth of 8.0% q-o-q. Growth on a y-o-y basis, however, contracted to 2.6% in Q2 2022 from 14.3% in Q1 2022.

In Q2 2022, issuance of central government bonds (including nontradable bonds) contracted substantially by 38.1% q-o-q as increased revenue collection in the first half of 2022 provided fiscal space for the government to reduce bond issuance. As a share of GDP, the government estimates the budget deficit will reach 3.9% this year, compared with an earlier forecast of 4.5%. The decline in issuance is also aligned with the government's commitment to bring the budget deficit back under its legal cap of 3.0% of GDP as allowed by

Table 1: Size and Composition of the Local Currency Bond Market in Indonesia

| | Outstanding Amount (billion) | | | | | | Growth Rate (%) | | | |
| | Q2 2021 | | Q1 2022 | | Q2 2022 | | Q2 2021 | | Q2 2022 | |
	IDR	USD	IDR	USD	IDR	USD	q-o-q	y-o-y	q-o-q	y-o-y
Total	4,912,250	339	5,478,441	381	5,497,153	369	2.4	30.6	0.3	11.9
Government	4,489,539	310	5,028,837	350	5,057,678	339	2.8	34.8	0.6	12.7
Central Govt. Bonds	4,282,623	295	4,828,648	336	4,848,083	325	3.1	37.9	0.4	13.2
of which: *Sukuk*	740,172	51	831,636	58	874,110	59	(3.3)	27.8	5.1	18.1
Nontradable Bonds	148,246	10	133,687	9	144,435	10	(5.0)	(15.8)	8.0	(2.6)
of which: *Sukuk*	33,106	2	26,324	2	26,374	2	(7.2)	(11.2)	0.2	(20.3)
Central Bank Bonds	58,670	4	66,501	5	65,160	4	6.8	18.2	(2.0)	11.1
of which: *Sukuk*	58,670	4	66,501	5	65,160	4	6.8	50.9	(2.0)	11.1
Corporate	422,711	29	449,604	31	439,474	29	(2.4)	(1.6)	(2.3)	4.0
of which: *Sukuk*	31,672	2	36,290	3	37,273	3	1.6	7.8	2.7	17.7

( ) = negative, IDR = Indonesian rupiah, q-o-q = quarter-on-quarter, Q1 = first quarter, Q2 =second quarter, USD = United States dollar, y-o-y = year-on-year.
Notes:
1. Bloomberg LP end-of-period local currency–USD rates are used.
2. Growth rates are calculated from local currency base and do not include currency effects.
3. *Sukuk* refers to Islamic bonds.
Sources: Bank Indonesia; Directorate General of Budget Financing and Risk Management, Ministry of Finance; Indonesia Stock Exchange; and Bloomberg LP.

Indonesian legislation. The limit was temporarily lifted during the pandemic due to the need for increased government spending to support the economy and provide for social relief and recovery measures.

Aside from Treasury bills and bonds, central government and nontradable bond issuances during the quarter included private placements and Savings Bond Ritel. The government raised a total of IDR13.9 trillion from the issuance of 2-year Savings Bond Ritel in June, which were sold to encourage individuals to invest in the bond market.

Central bank bonds. The stock of outstanding central bank bonds declined 2.0% q-o-q in Q2 2022, a turnaround from the 8.4% q-o-q growth in Q1 2022. The total amount of central bank bonds outstanding reached IDR65.2 trillion at the end of June, comprising solely Sukuk Bank Indonesia. Issuance of Sukuk Bank Indonesia totaled IDR331.9 trillion in Q2 2022, posting a contraction of 12.5% q-o-q.

Corporate bonds. At the end of June, the size of Indonesia's corporate bond market stood at IDR439.5 trillion, declining 2.3% q-o-q in Q2 2022 after posting a 4.5% q-o-q expansion in Q1 2022. The decline in the corporate bond stock stemmed from reduced issuance of corporate bonds in Q2 2022 amid uncertainties in the economic outlook. At only 8.0% of the total bond stock, Indonesia's LCY corporate bond market accounts for the smallest share of the overall market among emerging East Asian peers.

The aggregate bonds outstanding of the 30 largest corporate bond issuers in Indonesia amounted to IDR308.8 trillion at the end of June, representing 70.3% of the total corporate bond market (**Table 2**). The top 30 list includes 15 firms from the banking and financial sectors. The remaining 15 institutions are engaged in highly capitalized sectors such as energy, manufacturing, telecommunications, and construction. More than half of the top 30 list are state-owned entities (17 companies).

The top five corporate bond issuers in Indonesia, all of which are state-owned firms except for one, maintained their rankings in Q2 2022 from the preceding quarter. Leading the list was Perusahaan Listrik Negara with outstanding bonds of IDR34.5 trillion for a 7.8% share of the corporate bond total at the end of June.

Next was financing firm Indonesia Eximbank whose IDR18.8 trillion of bonds accounted for a 4.3% share of the corporate total. Third on the list was Indah Kiat Pulp and Paper with total outstanding bonds of IDR17.0 trillion and a 3.9% share. At the fourth and fifth spots were Bank Rakyat Indonesia and Sarana Multi Infrastruktur with market shares of 3.5% and 3.4%, respectively. All other firms on the list had a share of 3.1% or less of the total corporate bond stock.

Corporate bond sales during the quarter tallied IDR30.5 trillion, down by 21.4% q-o-q in Q2 2022 and a reversal from the 24.0% q-o-q hike in Q1 2022. Unfavorable market conditions caused by volatility in financial markets, which tends to result in higher borrowing costs, has led some corporates to delay planned bond issuances. Nonetheless, there were 16 firms who tapped the bond market in Q2 2022 for funding to support capital expenditures and refinance maturing obligations.

A total of 44 corporate bond series were added to the corporate bond stock in Q2 2022, eight of which were structured as *sukuk*. There were two series of *sukuk ijarah* (Islamic bonds backed by lease agreements) and six series of *sukuk mudharabah* (Islamic bonds backed by a profit-sharing scheme from a business venture or partnership).

Among the new issuance during the quarter, the most common bond maturity was 3 years (16 series) and 5 years (15 series), which accounted for 36.4% and 34.1%, respectively, of the issuance total in Q2 2022. The shortest-dated bond issued in Q2 2022 was for 367 days, issued by Adhi Commuter Properti, while the longest was for a 7-year duration.

The five largest corporate bond issuances in Q2 2022 were all from state-owned institutions (**Table 3**). Bank Negara Indonesia was the largest issuer with total issuance of IDR5.0 trillion from a dual-tranche sale of conventional green bonds. It was followed by pawnshop firm Pegadaian, which raised an aggregate of IDR4.0 trillion from the sale of two series of conventional bonds and two series of *sukuk mudharabah*. At the third spot was Adhi Karya, which sold a total IDR3.8 trillion from three series of bonds. Next were Waskita Karya and Permodalan Nasional Madani, which raised IDR3.3 trillion and IDR3.0 trillion, respectively.

Table 2: Top 30 Issuers of Local Currency Corporate Bonds in Indonesia

	Issuers	Outstanding Amount		State-Owned	Listed Company	Type of Industry
		LCY Bonds (IDR billion)	LCY Bonds (USD billion)			
1.	Perusahaan Listrik Negara	34,489	2.32	Yes	No	Energy
2.	Indonesia Eximbank	18,789	1.26	Yes	No	Finance
3.	Indah Kiat Pulp & Paper	16,993	1.14	No	Yes	Pulp and Paper
4.	Bank Rakyat Indonesia	15,501	1.04	Yes	Yes	Banking
5.	Sarana Multi Infrastruktur	15,031	1.01	Yes	No	Finance
6.	Permodalan Nasional Madani	13,522	0.91	Yes	No	Finance
7.	Bank Mandiri	11,900	0.80	Yes	Yes	Banking
8.	Sarana Multigriya Finansial	11,865	0.80	Yes	No	Finance
9.	Waskita Karya	11,395	0.76	Yes	Yes	Building Construction
10.	Pegadaian	10,297	0.69	Yes	No	Finance
11.	Bank Tabungan Negara	10,277	0.69	Yes	Yes	Banking
12.	Astra Sedaya Finance	10,242	0.69	No	No	Finance
13.	Wijaya Karya	10,000	0.67	Yes	Yes	Building Construction
14.	Hutama Karya	9,313	0.63	Yes	No	Nonbuilding Construction
15.	Pupuk Indonesia	9,046	0.61	Yes	No	Chemical Manufacturing
16.	Merdeka Copper Gold	8,318	0.56	No	Yes	Mining
17.	Bank Negara Indonesia	8,000	0.54	Yes	Yes	Banking
18.	Bank Pan Indonesia	7,802	0.52	No	Yes	Banking
19.	Tower Bersama Infrastructure	7,663	0.51	No	Yes	Telecommunications Infrastructure Provider
20.	OKI Pulp & Paper Mills	7,500	0.50	No	No	Pulp and Paper Manufacturing
21.	Adira Dinamika Multi Finance	7,325	0.49	No	Yes	Finance
22.	Indosat	7,194	0.48	No	Yes	Telecommunications
23.	Sinar Mas Agro Resources and Technology	6,603	0.44	No	Yes	Food
24.	Chandra Asri Petrochemical	6,500	0.44	No	Yes	Petrochemicals
25.	Bank Pembangunan Daerah Jawa Barat Dan Banten	6,413	0.43	Yes	Yes	Banking
26.	Lontar Papyrus Pulp & Paper Industry	6,000	0.40	No	No	Pulp and Paper Manufacturing
27.	Bank CIMB Niaga	5,606	0.38	No	Yes	Banking
28.	Federal International Finance	5,267	0.35	No	No	Finance
29.	Adhi Karya	5,187	0.35	Yes	Yes	Building Construction
30.	Telkom Indonesia	4,800	0.32	Yes	Yes	Telecommunications
	Total Top 30 LCY Corporate Issuers	**308,838**	**20.73**			
	Total LCY Corporate Bonds	**439,474**	**29.50**			
	Top 30 as % of Total LCY Corporate Bonds	**70.3%**	**70.3%**			

IDR = Indonesian rupiah, LCY = local currency, USD = United States dollar.
Notes:
1. Data as of 30 June 2022.
2. State-owned firms are defined as those in which the government has more than a 50% ownership stake.
Source: *AsianBondsOnline* calculations based on Indonesia Stock Exchange data.

Table 3: Notable Local Currency Corporate Bond Issuances in the Second Quarter of 2022

Corporate Issuers	Coupon Rate (%)	Issued Amount (IDR billion)
Bank Negara Indonesia		
3-year bond	6.35	4,000
5-year bond	6.85	1,000
Pegadaian		
370-day bond	3.60	2,431
370-day sukuk mudharabah	3.60	671
3-year bond	5.35	598
3-year sukuk mudharabah	5.35	320
Adhi Karya		
3-year bond	8.25	1,286
5-year bond	9.00	668
7-year bond	10.20	1,796
Waskita Karya		
5-year bond	6.65	658
5-year sukuk mudharabah	6.65	383
7-year bond	7.55	1,469
7-year sukuk mudharabah	7.55	765
Permodalan Nasional Madani		
370-day bond	3.75	2,374
3-year bond	5.30	626

IDR = Indonesian rupiah.
Note: Sukuk mudharabah are Islamic bonds backed by a profit-sharing scheme from a business venture or partnership.
Source: Indonesia Stock Exchange.

Investor Profiles

The foreign sell-off continued in the Indonesian LCY bond market in Q2 2022, which recorded net outflows of USD4.6 billion versus USD2.9 billion in Q1 2022. Market volatility arising from aggressive rate hikes by the Federal Reserve and the broad strengthening of the US dollar led offshore investors to dump IDR-denominated bonds. The foreign holdings share dropped to 16.1% at the end of June from 17.6% at the end of March and from 22.8% at the end of June 2021 (**Figure 2**). In nominal terms, foreign bond holdings fell significantly by 20.2% y-o-y to IDR780.2 trillion at the end of June.

About 63.1% of bonds held by foreign investors carried maturities of over 5 years or longer (**Figure 3**). This share was down from 68.4% at the end of December. Bonds with maturities of more than 2 years to 5 years comprised 22.1% of the aggregate holdings of foreign investors, which also constituted a decline from a 23.8% share at the end of December. On the other hand, the share of bonds with maturities of 2 years or less increased from a 7.8% share at the end of December to 14.8% at the end of June. This indicated a shift in the risk preference of offshore holders toward shorter-term maturities amid heightened uncertainties over the global growth outlook and persistent inflation.

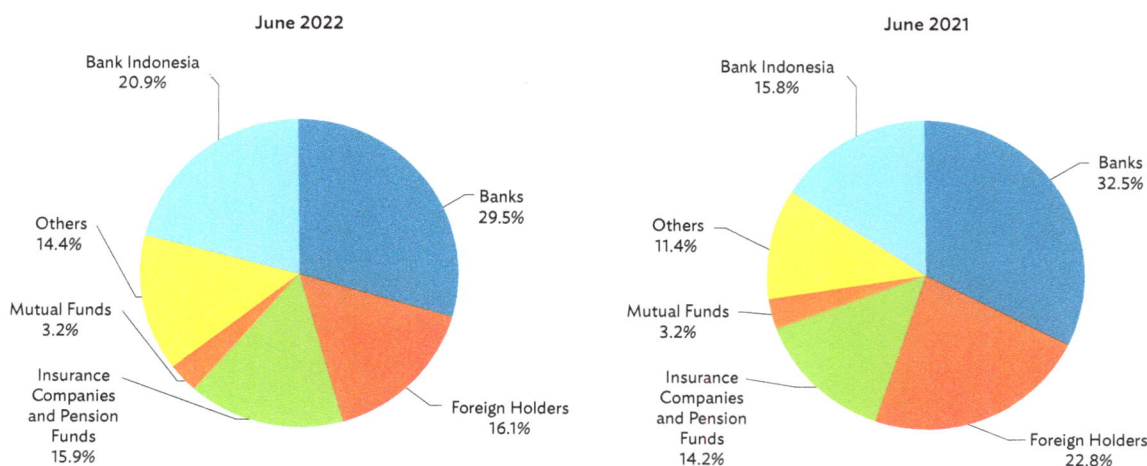

Figure 2: Local Currency Central Government Bonds Investor Profile

Source: Directorate General of Budget Financing and Risk Management, Ministry of Finance.

Figure 3: Foreign Holdings of Local Currency Central Government Bonds by Maturity

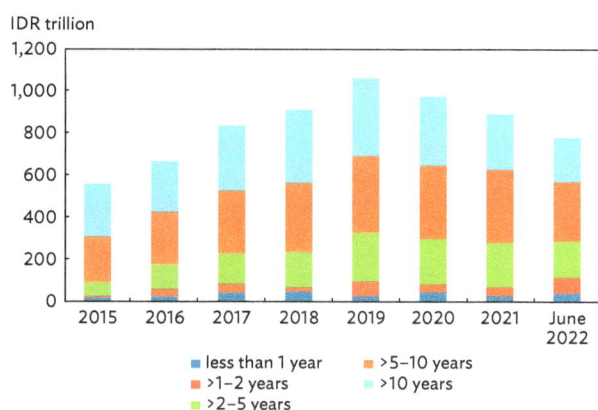

IDR = Indonesian rupiah.
Source: Directorate General of Budget Financing and Risk Management, Ministry of Finance.

As in previous quarters, domestic investors supported the bond market. Banks remained the largest investor group, accounting for 29.5% of total government bonds at the end of June. This, however, was down from banks' 32.5% share in the same period a year earlier.

All other investor groups recorded increases in their respective holdings of LCY government bonds at the end of June. Bank Indonesia recorded the biggest increase, as its holdings share rose 5.1 percentage points to 20.9% at the end of June. Amid volatile market conditions that resulted in the partial award of bonds during Q2 2022 Treasury auctions, Bank Indonesia purchased bonds as part of its burden-sharing agreement with the government to help stabilize financial markets and support fiscal measures. From 1 January to 22 August, the government bond purchases of Bank Indonesia amounted to IDR58.3 trillion.

The next largest expansion in shareholdings was seen for the "other investors" group, which includes individuals and corporations, among others. This group's shareholdings climbed 2.9 percentage points to reach 14.4% at the end of June. The bond holdings of insurance and pension funds rose 1.7 percentage points to a 15.9% share during the same period, while the holdings of mutual funds remained stable at 3.2%.

Ratings Update

On 27 July, Japan Credit Rating Agency affirmed Indonesia's sovereign credit rating at BBB+ with a stable outlook. The rating agency cited Indonesia's strong domestic-demand-led growth potential, restrained public debt, and resilience to external shocks as factors for the ratings affirmation. The rating agency views that economic recovery will be on track for GDP growth to exceed 5.0% in 2022, supported by expansions in private consumption, investments, and exports.

Policy, Institutional, and Regulatory Developments

Bank Indonesia Begins to Unwind Its Holdings of Government Bonds

In July, Bank Indonesia began to unwind its holdings of government bonds in the secondary market. The bonds that will be sold include government bonds with maturities of up to 5 years, which the central bank had accumulated under its burden-sharing agreement with the government during the pandemic. This move is part of the central bank's preemptive mitigation measures to combat inflationary pressure and strengthen the domestic currency.

State Budget 2023 Aims to Return Budget Deficit to Below 3.0% of Gross Domestic Product

In August, the President of Indonesia announced the government's commitment to reduce the budget deficit to within the legal cap of 3.0% of GDP in 2023. The government's proposed 2023 state budget sets state revenues at IDR2,443.6 trillion and state expenditures at IDR3,041.7 trillion. Debt financing is projected to decline to IDR696.3 trillion. The 2023 state budget is guided by the following macroeconomic assumptions: (i) economic growth of 5.3%, (ii) inflation of 3.3%, and (iii) an exchange rate of IDR14,750 per USD1.0.

Republic of Korea

Yield Movements

The Republic of Korea's LCY government bond yield curve flattened between 15 June and 15 August as yields for short-term bonds rose while those for the rest of the curve fell (**Figure 1**). Yields for tenors of between 3 months and 1 year rose 36 basis points (bps) on average, with the 3-month tenor posting the largest increase at 43 bps. Meanwhile, yields for the 2-year through 10-year tenors fell 48 bps on average, with the 5-year tenor posting the largest increase of 58 bps. Yields for the 20-year to 50-year tenors fell 34 bps on average. The spread between the 10-year and 2-year tenors narrowed to 14 bps from 26 bps during the review period.

Yields rose at the short-end of the curve, reflecting the recent rate hikes and expectations of further policy tightening by both the Bank of Korea and the United States (US) Federal Reserve. At its 13 July and 25 August meetings, the Bank of Korea raised the base rate by 50 bps and 25 bps, respectively, to 2.50% to arrest the acceleration in inflation. This brought cumulative rate hikes for the year to 150 basis points. Inflation quickened to 6.3% year-on-year (y-o-y) in July, a more than 20-year high from quarterly averages of 3.8% y-o-y and 5.4% y-o-y, respectively, in the first quarter (Q1) and second quarter (Q2) of 2022, due to the continued rise in commodity prices and supply disruptions. Upward pressure on yields also stemmed from the aggressive monetary policy tightening of the Federal Reserve, which raised the federal funds rate target range by 75 bps each at its June and July monetary policy meetings to a range of 2.25%–2.50%.

The decline in long-term yields reflects concerns of a global and domestic economic slowdown. Downside risks have been exacerbated by the sharp weakening of the Korean won, making imports costly and further dampening private consumption, and an economic slowdown in the People's Republic of China, which is a major trade partner of the Republic of Korea. At its 25 August monetary policy meeting, the Bank of Korea lowered its full-year 2022 and 2023 economic growth forecasts to 2.6% and 2.1%, respectively, from May forecasts of 2.7% and 2.4%, primarily due to weakening exports. Meanwhile, inflation is projected to be 5.2% in 2022 and 3.7% in 2023, higher than May forecasts of 4.5% and 2.9%.

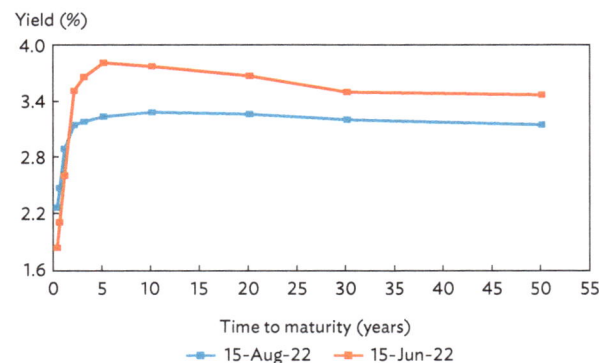

Figure 1: The Republic of Korea's Benchmark Yield Curve—Local Currency Government Bonds

Source: Based on data from Bloomberg LP.

The Republic of Korea's economic growth slowed further to 2.9% y-o-y in Q2 2022 from 3.0% y-o-y in Q1 2022 and 4.2% y-o-y in the fourth quarter of 2021, based on preliminary estimates by the Bank of Korea. The lower growth was primarily driven by the continued contraction of 2.9% y-o-y in gross fixed capital formation in Q2 2022, following a 3.5% y-o-y decline in the previous quarter. Both private and public consumption posted smaller annual increases in Q2 2022 at 3.9% y-o-y and 3.7% y-o-y, respectively, from 4.3% y-o-y and 6.6% y-o-y in Q1 2022. Export growth also decelerated to 4.6% y-o-y in Q2 2022 from 7.3% y-o-y in the previous quarter. On a quarter-on-quarter (q-o-q) basis, domestic economic growth inched up to 0.7% in Q2 2022 from 0.6% in the previous quarter.

Aggressive tightening by the Federal Reserve and a stronger US dollar led to a sell-off in bond markets across the region. The rise in US Treasury yields resulted in a decline in the spread and eventually an interest rate inversion between the US and Korean markets, making domestic bonds less attractive. Net foreign inflows into the Republic of Korea's LCY bond market declined to KRW36 billion in April before recovering to KRW1,370 billion in May. In June, the Republic of Korea registered net outflows of KRW934 billion following the 75 bps rate hike by the Federal Reserve. The declining monthly net inflows (and ultimately, net outflows) were also largely driven by the continued depreciation of the Korean won, which reached a low of USD1,326.2 per

USD1.0 on 15 July, representing a 10.3% depreciation from the start of the year despite market intervention by the Bank of Korea to support the currency. In July, foreign investors returned to the market with net inflows of KRW3,561 billion, as market participants expected a slowdown in the Federal Reserve policy tightening.

Size and Composition

The Republic of Korea's LCY bonds outstanding inched up 1.0% quarter-on-quarter (q-o-q) to reach KRW2,925.7 trillion (USD2,252.7 billion) at the end of June, which was slower than the 2.0% q-o-q posted in the previous quarter (**Table 1**). Growth was largely driven by the government segment as the corporate sector posted only minimal growth. On an annual basis, the size of the Republic of Korea's LCY bond market rose 6.1% y-o-y, compared with a 7.5% y-o-y increase posted in Q1 2022.

Government bonds. The Republic of Korea's LCY government bond market expanded 1.6% q-o-q in Q2 2022 to KRW1,242.0 trillion, down from the 3.4% q-o-q growth in the previous quarter. This was mostly due to the high base in Q1 2022 when the government frontloaded its issuance to meet budgeting needs. Growth for the quarter was mainly driven by the 3.4% q-o-q rise in the stock of central government bonds, while the amount of central bank bonds declined 10.2% q-o-q. Meanwhile, other government bonds rose 1.9% q-o-q during the quarter.

Issuance of government bonds rose 4.9% q-o-q to KRW102.9 trillion in Q2 2022, driven by the 37.8% q-o-q increase in bond issuance from government-owned entities. Central government bonds issuance also rose but at a slower pace of 9.7% q-o-q in Q2 2022. Meanwhile, issuance of Monetary Stabilization Bonds by the Bank of Korea fell 21.2% q-o-q. The Bank of Korea scaled down issuance of these bonds beginning in late 2021 to ease yield volatility, as the central bank was already tightening liquidity via policy rate hikes.

Corporate bonds. The outstanding size of the Republic of Korea's LCY corporate bond market posted a marginal increase of 0.5% q-o-q to reach KRW1,683.8 trillion (USD1,296.4 billion) at the end of June, which was lower than the 1.0% q-o-q increase posted in the previous quarter. **Table 2** lists the top 30 LCY corporate bond issuers in the Republic of Korea, with aggregate bonds outstanding of KRW998.5 trillion at the end of June, comprising 59.3% of the total LCY corporate bond market. Financial institutions involved in banking and securities investments continued to dominate the list with a collective share of 63.2%. Korea Housing Finance Corporation, a government-related institution providing financial assistance for social housing, remained the single-largest corporate bond issuer with outstanding bonds of KRW151.2 trillion. Industrial Bank of Korea and Korea Investment and Securities followed with total bonds outstanding of KRW73.4 trillion and KRW53.0 trillion, respectively.

Table 1: Size and Composition of the Local Currency Bond Market in the Republic of Korea

| | Outstanding Amount (billion) | | | | | | Growth Rate (%) | | | |
| | Q2 2021 | | Q1 2022 | | Q2 2022 | | Q2 2021 | | Q2 2022 | |
	KRW	USD	KRW	USD	KRW	USD	q-o-q	y-o-y	q-o-q	y-o-y
Total	2,756,445	2,448	2,898,057	2,391	2,925,746	2,253	2.3	7.9	1.0	6.1
Government	1,158,252	1,029	1,222,359	1,009	1,241,968	956	3.2	11.6	1.6	7.2
Central Government Bonds	807,725	717	884,103	730	914,183	704	5.0	19.0	3.4	13.2
Central Bank Bonds	154,230	137	140,190	116	125,910	97	(1.9)	(8.7)	(10.2)	(18.4)
Others	196,297	174	198,065	163	201,875	155	0.3	3.2	1.9	2.8
Corporate	1,598,193	1,419	1,675,698	1,383	1,683,778	1,296	1.6	5.4	0.5	5.4

( ) = negative, KRW = Korean won, q-o-q = quarter-on-quarter, Q1 = first quarter, Q2 = second quarter, USD = United States dollar, y-o-y = year-on-year.
Notes:
1. Bloomberg LP end-of-period local currency–USD rates are used.
2. Growth rates are calculated from local currency base and do not include currency effects.
3. "Others" comprise Korea Development Bank Bonds, National Housing Bonds, and Seoul Metro Bonds.
4. Corporate bonds include equity-linked securities and derivatives-linked securities.
Sources: The Bank of Korea and KG Zeroin Corporation.

Table 2: Top 30 Issuers of Local Currency Corporate Bonds in the Republic of Korea

	Issuers	Outstanding Amount		State-Owned	Listed on		Type of Industry
		LCY Bonds (KRW billion)	LCY Bonds (USD billion)		KOSPI	KOSDAQ	
1.	Korea Housing Finance Corporation	151,207	116.4	Yes	No	No	Housing Finance
2.	Industrial Bank of Korea	73,360	56.5	Yes	Yes	No	Banking
3.	Korea Investment and Securities	52,999	40.8	No	No	No	Securities
4.	Meritz Securities	49,640	38.2	No	Yes	No	Securities
5.	Hana Securities	48,548	37.4	No	No	No	Securities
6.	Mirae Asset Securities	48,480	37.3	No	Yes	No	Securities
7.	Shinhan Investment Corporation	48,422	37.3	No	No	No	Securities
8.	Korea Electric Power Corporation	45,940	35.4	Yes	Yes	No	Electricity, Energy, and Power
9.	KB Securities	45,631	35.1	No	No	No	Securities
10.	NH Investment & Securities	34,568	26.6	Yes	Yes	No	Securities
11.	Korea Land & Housing Corporation	32,577	25.1	Yes	No	No	Real Estate
12.	Shinhan Bank	28,445	21.9	No	No	No	Banking
13.	The Export-Import Bank of Korea	27,690	21.3	Yes	No	No	Banking
14.	Korea Expressway	27,430	21.1	Yes	No	No	Transport Infrastructure
15.	Samsung Securities	26,091	20.1	No	Yes	No	Securities
16.	Woori Bank	23,860	18.4	Yes	Yes	No	Banking
17.	KEB Hana Bank	23,111	17.8	No	No	No	Banking
18.	NongHyup Bank	21,880	16.8	Yes	No	No	Banking
19.	Kookmin Bank	21,044	16.2	No	No	No	Banking
20.	Korea SMEs and Startups Agency	20,298	15.6	Yes	No	No	SME Development
21.	Korea National Railway	19,320	14.9	Yes	No	No	Transport Infrastructure
22.	Shinhan Card	17,220	13.3	No	No	No	Credit Card
23.	Shinyoung Securities	16,004	12.3	No	Yes	No	Securities
24.	Hyundai Capital Services	15,680	12.1	No	No	No	Consumer Finance
25.	Hanwha Investment and Securities	14,773	11.4	No	No	No	Securities
26.	KB Kookmin Bank Card	14,245	11.0	No	No	No	Consumer Finance
27.	Standard Chartered Bank Korea	13,710	10.6	No	No	No	Banking
28.	NongHyup	12,830	9.9	Yes	No	No	Banking
29.	Samsung Card Co.	12,248	9.4	No	Yes	No	Credit Card
30.	Korea Railroad Corporation	11,230	8.6	Yes	No	No	Transport Infrastructure
	Total Top 30 LCY Corporate Issuers	**998,481**	**769**				
	Total LCY Corporate Bonds	**1,683,778**	**1,296.4**				
	Top 30 as % of Total LCY Corporate Bonds	**59.3%**	**59.3%**				

KOSDAQ = Korean Securities Dealers Automated Quotations, KOSPI = Korea Composite Stock Price Index, KRW = Korean won, LCY = local currency, SMEs = small and medium-sized enterprises, USD = United States dollar.
Notes:
1. Data as of 30 June 2022.
2. State-owned firms are defined as those in which the government has more than a 50% ownership stake.
3. Corporate bonds include equity-linked securities and derivatives-linked securities.
Sources: *AsianBondsOnline* calculations based on Bloomberg LP and KG Zeroin Corporation data.

Corporate bond issuance rose 5.7% y-o-y to KRW143.3 trillion in Q2 2022 from KRW135.5 trillion in the previous quarter. Issuance remained tepid in Q2 2022 due to continued yield volatility amid the monetary policy tightening by both the Bank of Korea and the Federal Reserve. **Table 3** lists the notable corporate bond issuances in Q2 2022, including from financial firms such as Industrial Bank of Korea, Export–Import Bank of Korea, Kookmin Bank, and NongHyup Bank.

Investor Profile

Insurance companies and pension funds remained the top holders of the Republic of Korea's LCY government bonds at the end of March, comprising 33.0% of the market (**Figure 2**). However, this was down from 34.7% in Q1 2021, as the share of banks rose to 21.4% from 18.3% during the review period. The shares of general government and other financial institutions also fell in

Table 3: Notable Local Currency Corporate Bond Issuances in the Second Quarter of 2022

Corporate Issuers	Coupon Rate (%)	Issued Amount (KRW billion)
Industrial Bank of Korea[a]		
5-month bond	–	400
7-month bond	3.03	480
7-month bond	3.03	320
1-year bond	2.92	360
2-year bond	3.77	410
5-year bond	4.13	590
Export–Import Bank of Korea[a]		
2-month bond	–	350
1-year bond	3.04	490
1-year bond	3.01	490
1-year bond	–	390
1-year bond	2.92	340
1-year bond	–	290

Corporate Issuers	Coupon Rate (%)	Issued Amount (KRW billion)
Kookmin Bank[a]		
1-month bond	3.14	620
1-year bond	3.26	440
1-year bond	2.45	360
1.3-year bond	3.14	450
1.5-year bond	2.82	480
NongHyup Bank[a]		
1-year bond	2.92	510
1-year bond	2.92	480
1-year bond	2.92	340
1-year bond	2.92	290
1.5-year bond	2.71	290

– = not available, KRW = Korean won.
[a] Multiple issuance of the same tenor indicates issuance on different dates.
Source: Based on data from Bloomberg LP.

Figure 2: Local Currency Government Bonds Investor Profile

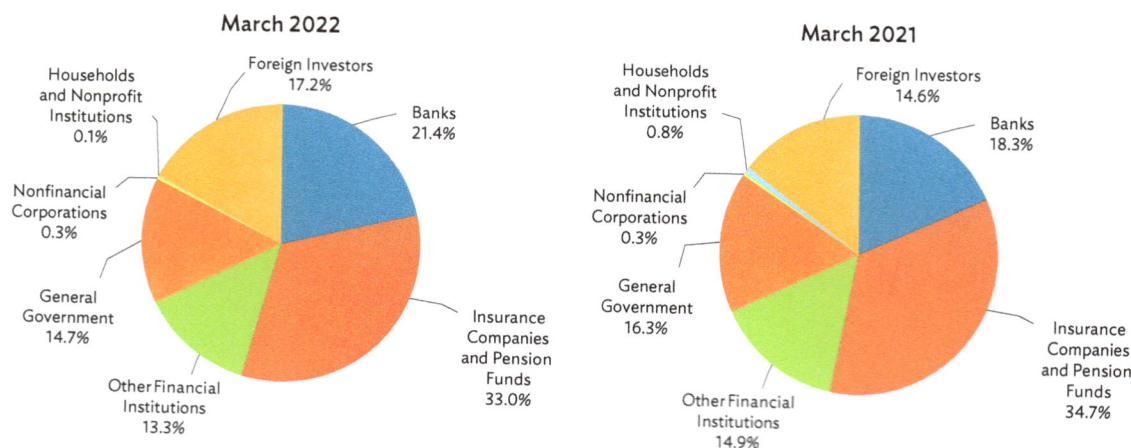

March 2022
- Foreign Investors 17.2%
- Banks 21.4%
- Insurance Companies and Pension Funds 33.0%
- Other Financial Institutions 13.3%
- General Government 14.7%
- Nonfinancial Corporations 0.3%
- Households and Nonprofit Institutions 0.1%

March 2021
- Foreign Investors 14.6%
- Banks 18.3%
- Insurance Companies and Pension Funds 34.7%
- Other Financial Institutions 14.9%
- General Government 16.3%
- Nonfinancial Corporations 0.3%
- Households and Nonprofit Institutions 0.8%

Source: *AsianBondsOnline* and The Bank of Korea.

Figure 5: Net Foreign Investment in Local Currency Bonds in the Republic of Korea by Remaining Maturity

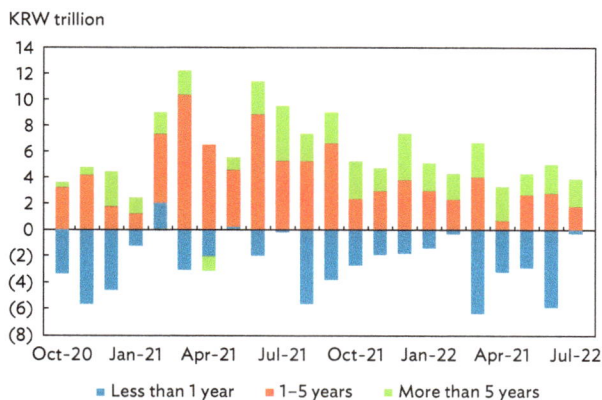

KRW = Korean won.
Source: Financial Supervisory Service.

Policy, Institutional, and Regulatory Developments

The Government Announces Plans to Improve Fiscal Soundness and Manage Global Economic Challenges

On 28 July, the Bank of Korea, Financial Services Commission, and Financial Supervisory Service held an emergency meeting to discuss the impact of the US Federal Open Market Committee's July meeting on the domestic financial market. Representatives from these institutions stated that the Republic of Korea's strong fundamentals and responses to the challenges had more impact on capital flows than the interest rate reversal between US Treasuries and domestic bonds, citing that Korean securities continued to register net foreign inflows in July. They also stated that the Republic of Korea is equipped to respond to these challenges, highlighting its high sovereign credit ratings and large foreign reserves. Nevertheless, the institutions will continue to monitor and increase the Republic of Korea's fiscal soundness and prepare preemptive measures and reforms to manage global economic challenges. These include, among others, (i) implementation of measures such as the government's emergency buyback of Korea Treasury Bonds (KTBs) and the Bank of Korea's buyback of KTBs in case of excessive volatility in the market; (ii) improvement of foreign investors' accessibility to domestic financial markets; and (iii) efforts for the Republic of Korea to join the FTSE World Government Bond Index via the introduction of a new tax scheme that will exempt income and corporate income tax on capital gains earned from nonresidents' and foreign corporations' investment in KTBs and central bank bonds.

Malaysia

Yield Movements

The yield curve for Malaysia's local currency (LCY) government bonds flattened between 15 June and 15 August (**Figure 1**). Short-term yields (from 1 month to 1 year) increased an average of 19 basis points (bps), while yields in the belly of the curve (2–5 years) fell an average of 14 bps, and longer term yields (6–30 years) declined an average of 44 bps. During the review period, the spread between the 10-year and 2-year government bond yields tightened from 90 bps to 61 bps.

The increase in short-term yields was due to the Bank Negara Malaysia's (BNM) decision to raise its overnight policy rate in July to combat inflationary pressure. The decline in long-term yields can be attributed to investors' attraction to the yields of Malaysian fixed-income securities amid market expectation of less aggressive moves by the United States Federal Reserve to tighten monetary policy. Malaysia has managed to keep its inflation rate in check, with yields of long-term bonds offering a buffer against rising inflation.

The Monetary Policy Committee of the BNM raised its policy rate to 2.25% from 2.00% on 6 July. The committee saw it fit to increase interest rates as a precautionary move to temper rising inflation due to the rising cost of and growing demand for commodities. The BNM also noted that the conditions that previously compelled the central bank to loosen its overnight policy rate in the midst of the coronavirus disease (COVID-19) pandemic had already subsided.

Malaysia's consumer price inflation saw an upward trend during the second quarter (Q2) of 2022. From 2.2% year-on-year (y-o-y) in March, price gains for basic goods and services accelerated each month during Q2 2022, logging inflation rates of 2.3% y-o-y and 2.8% y-o-y in April and May, respectively, before picking up to 3.4% y-o-y in June and 4.4% y-o-y in July. This brought average inflation for the first 7 months of 2022 to 2.8% y-o-y, well within the central bank's inflation forecast of between 2.2% and 3.2% for full-year 2022, leading to the BNM being less aggressive in hiking its policy rate compared to other central banks in the region.

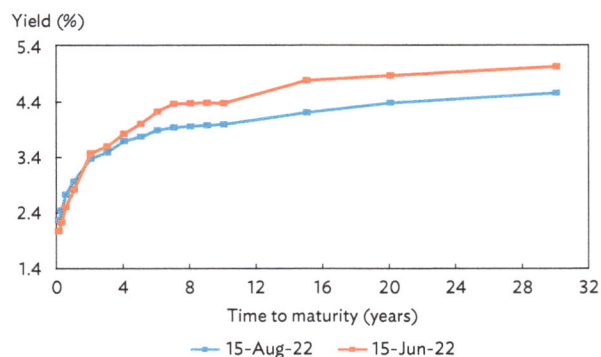

Figure 1: Malaysia's Benchmark Yield Curve—Local Currency Government Bonds

Source: Based on data from Bloomberg LP.

The gross domestic product of Malaysia expanded 8.9% y-o-y in Q2 2022, continuing the 5.0% y-o-y growth logged in the prior quarter, due to faster growth in the services and manufacturing sectors. The construction sector also rebounded after contracting in the first quarter (Q1) of 2022. A low base from Q2 2021, resulting from a complete movement control order, also contributed to the high annual economic growth. Year-to-date through June 2022, Malaysia's economic growth averaged 7.0% y-o-y, exceeding the BNM's expected annual growth rate of 5.3%–6.3% for full-year 2022.

Size and Composition

The Malaysian LCY bond market grew 2.3% quarter-on-quarter (q-o-q) in Q2 2022, attaining a size of MYR1,805.3 billion (USD409.5 billion) at the end of June, increasing from MYR1,764.9 billion at the end of the Q1 2022 (**Table 1**). Growth accelerated from the 1.7% q-o-q uptick logged in the previous quarter. On a y-o-y basis, the LCY bond market of Malaysia jumped 6.6% y-o-y, but down slightly from 7.0% y-o-y in Q1 2022. The bond market's growth in Q2 2022 was spurred by expansions in both outstanding LCY government and corporate bonds, which accounted for 56.3% and 43.7%, respectively, of total LCY bonds outstanding at the end of June. Total *sukuk* (Islamic bonds) outstanding reached MYR1,139.2 billion at the end of the review period, increasing 1.5% q-o-q. This growth was due to higher stocks of government and corporate *sukuk*.

Table 1: Size and Composition of the Local Currency Bond Market in Malaysia

| | Outstanding Amount (billion) | | | | | | Growth Rate (%) | | | |
| | Q2 2021 | | Q1 2022 | | Q2 2022 | | Q2 2021 | | Q2 2022 | |
	MYR	USD	MYR	USD	MYR	USD	q-o-q	y-o-y	q-o-q	y-o-y
Total	1,693	408	1,765	420	1,805	410	2.7	8.9	2.3	6.6
Government	924	223	976	232	1,016	230	3.9	11.5	4.1	9.9
Central Government Bonds	900	217	958	228	997	226	4.1	12.9	4.1	10.8
of which: Sukuk	415	100	455	108	470	107	2.9	12.9	3.3	13.4
Central Bank Bills	0	0	0	0	0.9	0.2	(100.0)	(100.0)	–	–
of which: Sukuk	0	0	0	0	0.2	0.05	–	–	–	–
Sukuk Perumahan Kerajaan	24	6	18	4	18	4	0.0	(10.1)	0.0	(24.9)
Corporate	769	185	789	188	790	179	1.3	6.0	0.1	2.6
of which: Sukuk	626	151	649	154	651	148	2.0	7.6	0.2	3.9

( ) = negative, – = not applicable, MYR = Malaysian ringgit, q-o-q = quarter-on-quarter, Q1 = first quarter, Q2 = second quarter, USD = United States dollar, y-o-y = year-on-year.
Notes:
1. Bloomberg LP end-of-period local currency–USD rates are used.
2. Growth rates are calculated from local currency base and do not include currency effects.
3. Sukuk refers to Islamic bonds.
4. Sukuk Perumahan Kerajaan are Islamic bonds issued by the Government of Malaysia to refinance funding for housing loans to government employees and to extend new housing loans.
Sources: Bank Negara Malaysia Fully Automated System for Issuing/Tendering and Bloomberg LP.

LCY bonds issued in Q2 2022 climbed 35.5% q-o-q to MYR110.3 billion from MYR81.4 billion in Q1 2022 as issuances of government and corporate bonds increased. This was a reversal from the contraction of 8.6% q-o-q logged in the preceding quarter.

Government bonds. Malaysia's LCY government bond market grew 4.1% q-o-q to a size of MYR1,015.8 billion at the end of Q1 2022. The increase was quicker than the growth of 2.8% q-o-q logged in the previous quarter. The LCY government bond market's growth was driven by a 4.1% q-o-q jump in outstanding central government bonds, which accounted for 98.1% of total outstanding LCY government bonds at the end of the review period. Central bank bills were issued again by the BNM during the quarter after inactivity since June 2021. The amount of outstanding Sukuk Perumahan Kerajaan at the end of Q2 2022 was the same as in the previous quarter.

LCY government bond issuance in Q2 2022 grew 33.7% q-o-q to MYR66.9 billion, due to increased issuances of Treasury bills and bonds, and central bank bills. The issuance of Malaysian Government Securities (conventional bonds) and Government Investment Issues (Islamic bonds) both jumped in Q2 2022 compared to the previous quarter.

Corporate bonds. Outstanding LCY corporate bonds marginally grew 0.1% q-o-q to MYR789.5 billion in Q2 2022, down from the 0.3% q-o-q growth registered in the prior quarter. Corporate sukuk outstanding inched up 0.2% q-o-q to MYR650.6 billion at the end of Q2 2022. This growth rate was lower than the 0.9% q-o-q growth recorded in Q1 2022.

The top 30 issuers of corporate bonds in Malaysia had a total of MYR468.5 billion worth of LCY corporate bonds outstanding at the end of the review period, corresponding to a share of 59.3% of total outstanding LCY corporate bonds (**Table 2**). DanaInfra Nasional, a state-owned company, had the most outstanding LCY corporate bonds at the end of Q2 2022, amounting to MYR80.0 billion. By sector, the biggest share among the top 30 list was comprised by financial institutions (50.6%) with MYR236.9 billion worth of outstanding LCY corporate bonds at the end of the review period.

LCY corporate bond issuance in Q2 2022 increased 38.3% q-o-q to MYR43.5 billion, reversing the 23.7% q-o-q contraction registered in Q1 2022. Companies brought forward their fundraising in anticipation of higher interest rates in the short-term due to monetary policy tightening in economies around the world.

At the end of June, electric utility company Tenaga Nasional issued five tranches of Islamic medium-term notes (MTNs) totaling MYR4.0 billion (**Table 3**). Drawn from the company's Islamic MTN program, the notes had tenors ranging from 7 years to

Table 2: Top 30 Issuers of Local Currency Corporate Bonds in Malaysia

	Issuers	Outstanding Amount		State-Owned	Listed Company	Type of Industry
		LCY Bonds (MYR billion)	LCY Bonds (USD billion)			
1.	DanaInfra Nasional	80.0	18.2	Yes	No	Finance
2.	Prasarana	39.7	9.0	Yes	No	Transport, Storage, and Communications
3.	Lembaga Pembiayaan Perumahan Sektor Awam	36.8	8.3	Yes	No	Property and Real Estate
4.	Cagamas	31.1	7.1	Yes	No	Finance
5.	Project Lebuhraya Usahasama	28.2	6.4	No	No	Transport, Storage, and Communications
6.	Urusharta Jamaah	27.3	6.2	Yes	No	Finance
7.	Perbadanan Tabung Pendidikan Tinggi Nasional	22.1	5.0	Yes	No	Finance
8.	Pengurusan Air	18.8	4.3	Yes	No	Energy, Gas, and Water
9.	Tenaga Nasional	16.8	3.8	No	Yes	Energy, Gas, and Water
10.	CIMB Group Holdings	13.5	3.1	Yes	No	Finance
11.	Maybank Islamic	13.0	2.9	No	Yes	Banking
12.	Malayan Banking	12.5	2.8	No	Yes	Banking
13.	Khazanah	10.9	2.5	Yes	No	Finance
14.	Sarawak Energy	10.8	2.4	Yes	No	Energy, Gas, and Water
15.	CIMB Bank	10.6	2.4	Yes	No	Finance
16.	Danum Capital	10.1	2.3	No	No	Finance
17.	Danga Capital	10.0	2.3	Yes	No	Finance
18.	Jimah East Power	8.7	2.0	Yes	No	Energy, Gas, and Water
19.	Public Bank	6.9	1.6	No	No	Banking
20.	Kuala Lumpur Kepong	6.6	1.5	No	Yes	Energy, Gas, and Water
21.	Sapura TMC	6.4	1.4	No	No	Finance
22.	Malaysia Rail Link	6.2	1.4	Yes	No	Construction
23.	Bakun Hydro Power Generation	5.5	1.3	No	No	Energy, Gas, and Water
24.	Bank Pembangunan Malaysia	5.5	1.2	Yes	No	Banking
25.	Turus Pesawat	5.3	1.2	Yes	No	Transport, Storage, and Communications
26.	YTL Power International	5.3	1.2	No	Yes	Energy, Gas, and Water
27.	GOVCO Holdings	5.1	1.2	Yes	No	Finance
28.	1Malaysia Development	5.0	1.1	Yes	No	Finance
29.	EDRA Energy	5.0	1.1	No	Yes	Energy, Gas, and Water
30.	Infracap Resources	4.9	1.1	Yes	No	Finance
Total Top 30 LCY Corporate Issuers		**468.5**	**106.3**			
Total LCY Corporate Bonds		**789.5**	**179.1**			
Top 30 as % of Total LCY Corporate Bonds		**59.3%**	**59.3%**			

LCY = local currency, MYR = Malaysian ringgit, USD = United States dollar.
Notes:
1. Data as of 30 June 2022.
2. State-owned firms are defined as those in which the government has more than a 50% ownership stake.
Source: *AsianBondsOnline* calculations based on Bank Negara Malaysia Fully Automated System for Issuing/Tendering data.

Table 3: Notable Local Currency Corporate Bond Issuances in the Second Quarter of 2022

Corporate Issuers	Coupon Rate (%)	Issued Amount (MYR million)
Tenaga Nasional		
7-year Islamic MTN	4.73	1,120.0
10-year Islamic MTN	4.84	300.0
15-year Islamic MTN	5.23	880.0
20-year Islamic MTN	5.36	500.0
25-year Islamic MTN	5.57	1,200.0
DanaInfra Nasional		
7-year Islamic MTN	3.99	415.0
10-year Islamic MTN	4.07	300.0
15-year Islamic MTN	4.53	870.0
20-year Islamic MTN	4.68	355.0
30-year Islamic MTN	4.80	560.0
Cagamas[a]		
2-year MTN	3.84	50.0
3-year Islamic MTN	3.92	555.0
3-year Islamic MTN	3.91	100.0
3-year Islamic MTN	4.00	150.0
5-year MTN	3.78	1,000.0

MTN = medium-term note, MYR = Malaysian ringgit.
[a] Multiple issuance of the same tenor indicates issuance on different dates.
Source: Bank Negara Malaysia Bond Info Hub.

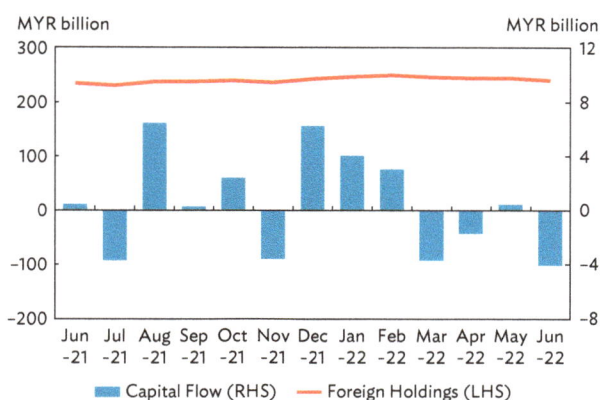

Figure 2: Foreign Holdings and Capital Flows in the Malaysian Local Currency Government Bond Market

LHS = left-hand side, MYR = Malaysian ringgit, RHS = right-hand side.
Notes:
1. Figures exclude foreign holdings of Bank Negara Malaysia bills.
2. Month-on-month changes in foreign holdings of local currency government bonds were used as a proxy for bond flows.
Source: Bank Negara Malaysia Monthly Statistical Bulletin.

25 years and coupon rates from 4.73% to 5.57%. In April, financial services company DanaInfra Nasional issued a five-tranche Islamic MTN worth MYR2.5 billion. With periodic distribution rates from 3.99% to 4.80%, the proceeds raised from the issuance will finance funding requirements of MRT line projects in Malaysia. Mortgage company Cagamas issued two MTNs in Q2 2022: a 2-year and a 5-year bond. Proceeds of the latter, which amounted to MYR1.0 billion, will be used to fund the purchase of housing loans. Cagamas also issued several 3-year Islamic MTNs with coupon rates ranging from 3.91% to 4.00%, the proceeds of which will be used to purchase home financing.

Investor Profile

Foreign investors reduced their holdings of Malaysian LCY government bonds in April, with the foreign-owned share of LCY government bonds declining to MYR243.5 billion from MYR245.2 billion in March (**Figure 2**). After a quick recovery to MYR244.0 billion in May, foreign holdings

dipped again to MYR239.9 billion in June. As a share of LCY government bonds, foreign holdings declined every month of the review period—from 25.2% at the end of April to 24.9% at the end of May and 24.1% at the end of June. Net capital outflows from the bond market were registered in April and June amounting to MYR1.7 billion and MYR4.1 billion, respectively. The net inflows of MYR0.5 billion in May were insufficient to offset these earlier outflows. The huge outflows in June were in line with outflows from emerging markets globally brought about by geopolitical risks, aggressive monetary policy tightening by the Federal Reserve, and inflation concerns worldwide.

At the end of March, the largest investors in LCY government bonds were financial institutions and social security institutions, with holdings of 34.5% and 27.7% of total outstanding bonds, respectively (**Figure 3**). The share of financial and social security institutions inched up from 34.0% and 27.3%, respectively, from the same period in 2021. Meanwhile, the share of foreign holders shrunk to 25.5% at the end of March from 25.7% a year prior. The holdings of insurance companies and the BNM were steady at 4.8% and 1.9%, respectively, between March 2021 and March 2022.

Figure 3: Local Currency Government Bonds Investor Profile

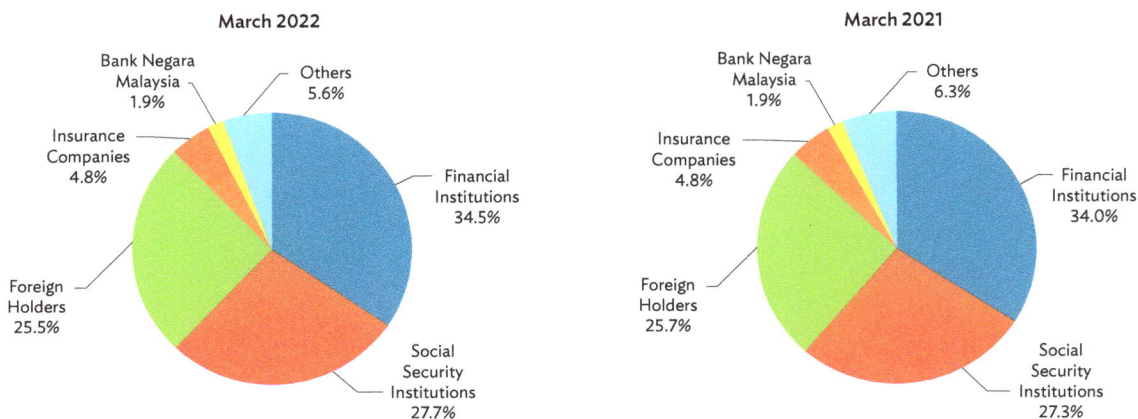

March 2022

March 2021

Note: "Others" include statutory bodies, nominees and trustee companies, and cooperatives and unclassified items.
Source: Bank Negara Malaysia.

Ratings Update

On 27 June, S&P Global Ratings revised its outlook for Malaysia's sovereign credit rating from negative to stable. At the same time, the rating agency affirmed the economy's credit rating of A–. The revision in outlook stemmed from S&P Global Ratings' view that Malaysia's economic growth momentum could be sustained in the next couple of years. It also reflected Malaysia's sustainable recovery spurred by its effective COVID-19 policy response. The affirmation of the credit rating was due to the Malaysia's strong external position, flexible monetary policy, and track record of achieving sustainable economic growth.

Policy, Institutional, and Regulatory Developments

Cagamas Conducts Maiden Issuance Based on Malaysia Overnight Rate

On 5 July, Cagamas, the national mortgage corporation of Malaysia issued the first floating-rate note referencing the Malaysia Overnight Rate (MYOR). Launched by the BNM in September 2021, MYOR is Malaysia's alternative reference rate to replace the London Interbank Offered Rate. MYOR is also transaction-based, allowing for a more robust reference rate and one that is reflective of active and liquid markets in Malaysia. To improve financial benchmarking in Malaysia, in March the BNM also launched the Malaysia Islamic Overnight Rate for Shariah-compliant financial products. Proceeds from Cagamas' floating-rate conventional MTN will be used to finance the purchase of housing loans from Malaysia's financial system.

Philippines

Yield Movements

The local currency (LCY) government bond yield curve in the Philippines flattened between 15 June and 15 August, as yields for short-dated tenors rose, while those for longer-dated maturities declined (**Figure 1**). Yields rose an average of 74 basis points (bps) for maturities of 2 years or less, with the largest increase seen in the 1-year tenor at 134 bps, followed by the 6-month tenor at 111 bps. In contrast, bond yields for maturities of 3 years or longer declined by an average of 49 bps during the review period. Yields fell the most for the 10-year maturity, which shed 101 bps. As the yield curve flattened, the spread of the 10-year over the 2-year maturity fell from 262 bps on 15 June to 132 bps on 15 August, the largest decline among emerging East Asia's bond markets.

The rise in yields at the shorter-end of the curve was largely driven by the monetary policy tightening stance of the Bangko Sentral ng Pilipinas (BSP). After raising policy rates by 25 bps each in May and June, the BSP hiked its rates by 75 bps in an off-cycle meeting on 14 July, which was followed by another 50 bps increase on 18 August. The BSP has become the most aggressive central bank in the region, raising rates consecutively since May for a total of 175 bps. The moves were largely in response to rising inflationary pressure. Consumer price inflation has steadily climbed since March of this year, rising at its fastest pace in July of 6.4% year-on-year (y-o-y), up from 6.1% y-o-y in June. In August, consumer price inflation slightly eased to 6.3% y-o-y. The BSP's revised forecast for full-year 2022 inflation is 5.4%, which exceeds its 2.0%–4.0% inflation rate target for the year.

On the other hand, the decline in yields for maturities of 3 years or longer was largely influenced by market expectations that the United States (US) Federal Reserve would adjust its monetary policy tightening stance to be less aggressive, fueled by a decline in global oil prices as well as a decline in July's US consumer price inflation and a negative reading for month-on-month producer price inflation. This was despite a still strong second quarter (Q2) gross domestic product (GDP) growth rate in the Philippines of 7.4% y-o-y versus 8.2% y-o-y in the first quarter (Q1) of 2022. The Philippines, however, continues to suffer from negative investor sentiment,

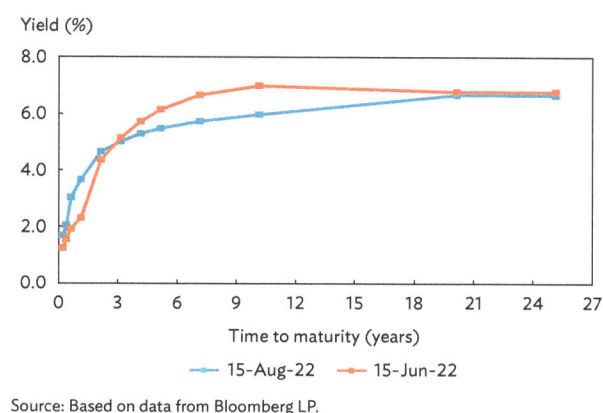

Figure 1: The Philippines' Benchmark Yield Curve— Local Currency Government Bonds

Source: Based on data from Bloomberg LP.

having consistently recorded foreign investor outflows from its stock market each month from March to July. For the January–July period, the Philippines also recorded negative outflows from its government bond market, though positive inflows were noted in the months of May, June, and July. This led the Philippine peso to depreciate significantly versus the US dollar by 9.1% year-to-date through 24 August.

Size and Composition

The size of the Philippines' LCY bond market reached PHP10,680.2 billion (USD194.3 billion) at the end of June, expanding at a modest pace of 2.4% quarter-on-quarter (q-o-q) in Q2 2022 versus 6.5% q-o-q in Q1 2022 (**Table 1**). The slowdown in the q-o-q growth was due to moderating growth in the government bond segment and a contraction in corporate bonds.

Government bonds. At the end of June, the outstanding amount of LCY government bonds climbed to PHP9,272.7 billion, with growth easing to 4.1% q-o-q in Q2 2022 from 6.5% q-o-q in the preceding quarter. The slower growth stemmed from a contraction in the stock of Treasury bills and a slower expansion in the stock of Treasury bonds. On the other hand, growth in the central bank bond stock moderated, while the stock of other government bonds posted strong growth during the review period.

Table 1: Size and Composition of the Local Currency Bond Market in the Philippines

| | Outstanding Amount (billion) | | | | | | Growth Rate (%) | | | |
| | Q2 2021 | | Q1 2022 | | Q2 2022 | | Q2 2021 | | Q2 2022 | |
	PHP	USD	PHP	USD	PHP	USD	q-o-q	y-o-y	q-o-q	y-o-y
Total	9,351	192	10,427	201	10,680	194	2.5	25.1	2.4	14.2
Government	7,834	160	8,911	172	9,273	169	3.9	32.7	4.1	18.4
Treasury Bills	1,023	21	657	13	544	10	(2.5)	28.4	(17.1)	(46.8)
Treasury Bonds	6,351	130	7,803	151	8,108	147	3.6	25.3	3.9	27.7
Central Bank Securities	400	8	410	8	567	10	34.5	–	38.3	41.8
Others	60	1	42	1	54	1	(9.1)	50.2	28.8	(10.3)
Corporate	1,517	31	1,515	29	1,408	26	(3.9)	(3.6)	(7.1)	(7.2)

( ) = negative, – = not applicable, PHP = Philippine peso, q-o-q = quarter-on-quarter, Q1 = first quarter, Q2 = second quarter, USD = United States dollar, y-o-y = year-on-year.
Notes:
1. Bloomberg end-of-period local currency–USD rates are used.
2. Growth rates are calculated from local currency base and do not include currency effects.
3. "Others" comprise bonds issued by government agencies, entities, and corporations for which repayment is guaranteed by the Government of the Philippines. This includes bonds issued by Power Sector Assets and Liabilities Management and the National Food Authority, among others.
4. Peso Global Bonds (PHP-denominated bonds payable in USD) are not included.
Sources: Bloomberg LP and Bureau of the Treasury.

The outstanding amount of Treasury bills dropped to PHP544.2 billion at the end of June, posting a contraction of 17.1% q-o-q and 46.8% y-o-y. The stock of Treasury bills declined as short-term interest rates continued to rise, stemming from the BSP's tightening monetary policy. Investors increasingly preferred longer maturities as yields continued to decline following the flattening of the Philippine yield curve. During the quarter, issuance of Treasury bills tallied PHP232.5 billion, up by 9.2% q-o-q. Despite increased issuance, the outstanding stock of Treasury bills declined due to a larger volume of maturities during the quarter.

On the other hand, Treasury bonds outstanding climbed to PHP8,107.7 billion, with growth easing to 3.9% q-o-q in Q2 2022 from 7.4% q-o-q in Q1 2022. Moderating growth in Treasury bonds was due to a relatively high base in the previous quarter as the Philippine government had issued Retail Treasury Bonds amounting to PHP457.8 billion in March, leading to a decline in government bond issuance in Q2 2022. During the quarter, issuance of Treasury bonds substantially declined by 55.8% q-o-q to PHP304.5 billion. Treasury bond and bill sales during the quarter fell below the Bureau of the Treasury's target of PHP650 billion.

Meanwhile, the BSP continued to post strong growth in its securities to mop up excess liquidity in the market to help curb inflationary pressure. The outstanding stock of central bank securities rose to PHP567.2 billion,

on slower growth of 38.3% q-o-q in Q2 2022 from 57.7% q-o-q in the prior quarter. Issuance of central bank instruments totaled PHP1,740.9 billion in Q2 2022, representing 76.0% of total government bond issuance during the quarter.

Corporate bonds. The corporate bond market's size reached PHP1,407.5 billion at the end of June on declines of 7.1% q-o-q and 7.2% y-o-y. Corporate bond issuance during the quarter declined 40.2% q-o-q, with total issuance reaching PHP91.2 billion due to higher borrowing costs. Uncertainties in the Philippine economic outlook and policy direction also dragged down issuance volume during the quarter.

By sectoral breakdown, corporate bonds outstanding largely comprised issuances from firms in the banking sector, with their share of the total dipping to 36.4% at the end of June from 41.0% a year earlier (**Figure 2**). Next were property firms, which saw their share inching up to 26.5% from 25.1% over the same period. Rising to the third spot were holdings firms, whose share climbed to 17.5% at the end of Q2 2022 from 13.8% a year earlier.

The 30 largest corporate bond issuers in the Philippines had an aggregate bond stock of PHP1,261.8 billion at the end of June, comprising 89.6% of the total corporate bond stock (**Table 2**). Compared with other markets, the Philippines' corporate bond market is relatively concentrated in a few large borrowers. Leading the list

Figure 2: Local Currency Corporate Bonds Outstanding by Sector

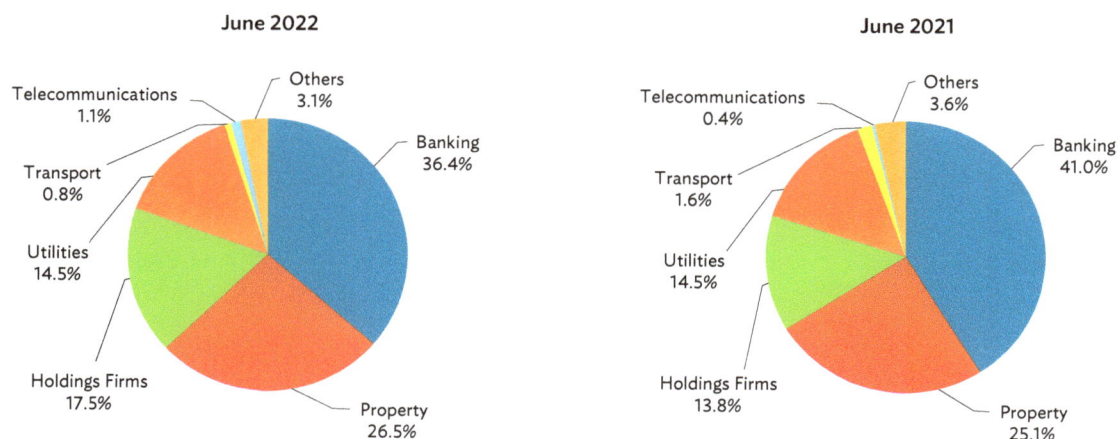

June 2022

Telecommunications 1.1%
Transport 0.8%
Utilities 14.5%
Holdings Firms 17.5%
Property 26.5%
Banking 36.4%
Others 3.1%

June 2021

Telecommunications 0.4%
Transport 1.6%
Utilities 14.5%
Holdings Firms 13.8%
Property 25.1%
Banking 41.0%
Others 3.6%

Source: Based on data from Bloomberg LP.

of top 30 was BDO Unibank with outstanding bonds of PHP126.6 billion and accounting for 9.0% of the corporate bond total. Next was SM Prime Holdings with bonds amounting to PHP119.6 billion and an 8.5% share of the corporate total. At the third spot was San Miguel with total bond size of PHP103.3 billion for a 7.3% share of the corporate total. Rounding out the fourth and fifth spots were Ayala Land and Metropolitan Bank, respectively, accounting for shares of 6.1% and 5.4% of the corporate bond market.

In Q2 2022, there were seven firms that tapped the Philippines' corporate bond market for funding. Total corporate bond issuance during the quarter comprised 13 new bond series. SM Prime Holdings had the largest aggregate issuance at PHP30.0 billion from the sale of 5-, 7-, and 10-year bonds in April (**Table 3**). Next was Ayala Corporation, which raised a total of PHP15.0 billion, followed by its sister company Ayala Land, which sold PHP12.0 billion worth of 6-year bonds. The shortest-dated bond issued during the quarter was a zero-coupon 6-month bond from Alsons Consolidated Resources. The longest-dated bond were 7-year issuances by both SM Prime Holdings and Ayala Corporation.

Investor Profile

For Q2 2022, banks and investment houses remained the largest investor in government bonds at the end of June with their share rising to 44.4% from 37.9% a year earlier (**Figure 3**). The holdings share of all other investors declined from that of the previous year. Investments by contractual savings institutions and tax-exempt institutions remained substantial, but their holdings shares fell to 33.5% in Q2 2022 from 35.4% in Q2 2021. The most dramatic decline came from brokers, custodians, and depositors whose share fell to 6.9% from 9.6% during the review period, largely as falling bond prices and rising US interest rates made Philippine assets less attractive.

Table 2: Top 30 Issuers of Local Currency Corporate Bonds in the Philippines

	Issuers	Outstanding Amount		State-Owned	Listed Company	Type of Industry
		LCY Bonds (PHP billion)	LCY Bonds (USD billion)			
1.	BDO Unibank	126.6	2.3	No	Yes	Banking
2.	SM Prime Holdings	119.6	2.2	No	Yes	Holding Firms
3.	San Miguel	103.3	1.9	No	Yes	Holding Firms
4.	Ayala Land	85.3	1.6	No	Yes	Property
5.	Metropolitan Bank	76.3	1.4	No	Yes	Banking
6.	Rizal Commercial Banking Corporation	62.8	1.1	No	No	Electricity, Energy, and Power
7.	SMC Global Power	60.0	1.1	No	Yes	Banking
8.	Aboitiz Power	60.0	1.1	No	Yes	Banking
9.	China Bank	51.6	0.9	No	Yes	Banking
10.	Security Bank	48.3	0.9	No	Yes	Electricity, Energy, and Power
11.	Ayala Corporation	45.0	0.8	No	Yes	Banking
12.	Petron	45.0	0.8	No	Yes	Electricity, Energy, and Power
13.	Vista Land	42.7	0.8	No	Yes	Property
14.	Filinvest Land	42.4	0.8	No	Yes	Holding Firms
15.	SM Investments	32.7	0.6	No	Yes	Holding Firms
16.	Bank of the Philippine Islands	30.1	0.5	No	Yes	Banking
17.	Union Bank of the Philippines	29.8	0.5	No	Yes	Property
18.	Aboitiz Equity Ventures	27.6	0.5	No	Yes	Holding Firms
19.	Philippine National Bank	22.9	0.4	No	Yes	Banking
20.	Maynilad	18.5	0.3	No	No	Water
21.	East West Banking	16.2	0.3	No	Yes	Banking
22.	Doubledragon	15.0	0.3	No	Yes	Banking
23.	San Miguel Food and Beverage	15.0	0.3	No	Yes	Property
24.	Robinsons Land	14.6	0.3	No	Yes	Food and Beverage
25.	Philippine Savings Bank	12.7	0.2	No	Yes	Property
26.	Bank of the Philippine Islands	12.2	0.2	No	Yes	Property
27.	Megaworld	12.0	0.2	No	Yes	Whole and Retail Trading
28.	Puregold	12.0	0.2	No	Yes	Holding Firms
29.	Metro Pacific Investments	11.4	0.2	No	Yes	Holding Firms
30.	GT Capital	10.1	0.2	No	No	Brewery
	Total Top 30 LCY Corporate Issuers	**1,261.8**	**23.0**			
	Total LCY Corporate Bonds	**1,407.5**	**25.6**			
	Top 30 as % of Total LCY Corporate Bonds	**89.6%**	**89.6%**			

LCY = local currency, PHP = Philippine peso, USD = United States dollar.
Notes:
1. Data as of 30 June 2022.
2. State-owned firms are defined as those in which the government has more than a 50% ownership stake.
Source: *AsianBondsOnline* calculations based on Bloomberg LP data.

Table 3: Notable Local Currency Corporate Bond Issuances in the Second Quarter of 2022

Corporate Issuers	Coupon Rate (%)	Issued Amount (PHP billion)
SM Prime Holdings		
5-year bond	5.61	10.92
7-year bond	6.12	13.03
10-year bond	6.54	6.05
Ayala Corporation		
3-year bond	4.45	5.00
5-year bond	5.62	7.50
7-year bond	6.14	2.50
Ayala Land		
6-year bond	5.81	12.00
Filinvest Land		
3-year bond	5.35	8.93
5-year bond	6.41	2.98
Union Bank of the Philippines		
1.5-year bond	3.25	11.00
Converge ICT Solutions		
5-year bond	5.59	10.00
Alsons Consolidated Resources		
0.5-year bond	0.00	0.27
1-year bond	0.00	1.00

PHP = Philippine peso.
Source: Based on data from Bloomberg LP.

Policy, Institutional, and Regulatory Developments

Bureau of the Treasury Releases Its July–August Borrowing Plan

The Bureau of the Treasury released its borrowing plan for July and August. The government planned to borrow PHP200 billion for the month of July, comprising PHP60 billion worth of Treasury bills and PHP140 billion worth of Treasury bonds with tenors ranging between 7 years and 14 years. For the month of August, the borrowing target was set at PHP215 billion: PHP75 billion in Treasury bills and PHP140 billion in Treasury bonds with tenors ranging from 3.5 years to 10 years.

Figure 3: Local Currency Government Bonds Investor Profile

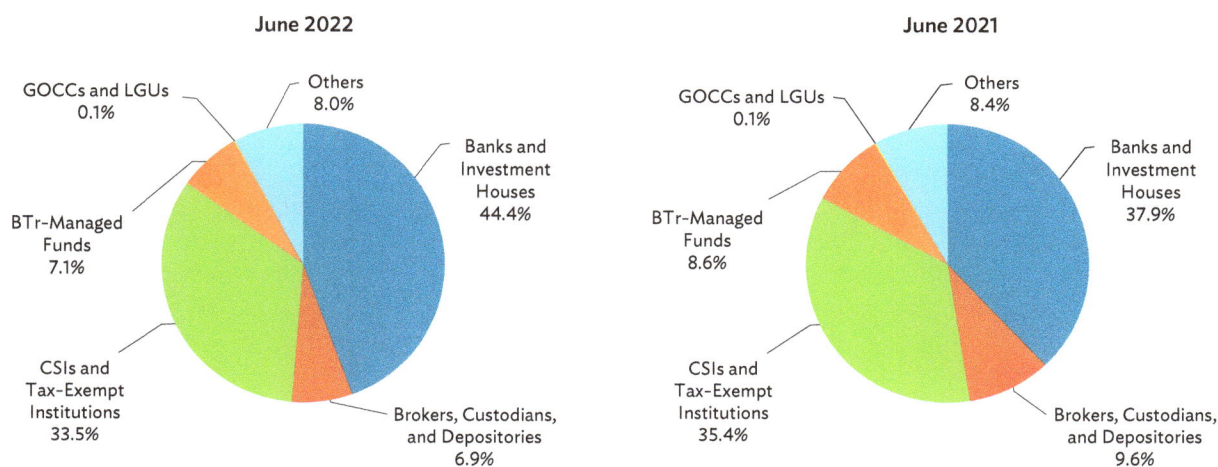

June 2022
- GOCCs and LGUs 0.1%
- Others 8.0%
- Banks and Investment Houses 44.4%
- BTr-Managed Funds 7.1%
- CSIs and Tax-Exempt Institutions 33.5%
- Brokers, Custodians, and Depositories 6.9%

June 2021
- GOCCs and LGUs 0.1%
- Others 8.4%
- Banks and Investment Houses 37.9%
- BTr-Managed Funds 8.6%
- CSIs and Tax-Exempt Institutions 35.4%
- Brokers, Custodians, and Depositories 9.6%

BTr = Bureau of the Treasury, CSI = contractual savings institution, GOCC = government-owned or -controlled corporation, LGU = local government unit.
Source: Bureau of the Treasury.

Singapore

Yield Movements

The local currency (LCY) government bond yield curve of Singapore flattened between 15 June and 15 August (**Figure 1**). On average, tenors from 3 months to 1 year jumped 75 basis points (bps), while longer-term tenors (from 5 years to 20 years) declined an average of 47 bps. During the review period, the yield spread between 10-year and 2-year government bonds contracted from 57 bps to 2 bps.

The increased short-term yields was due to Monetary Authority of Singapore (MAS) tightening its monetary policy in July as a preventive measure against inflationary pressure. The flight to safety amid continued uncertainties in the trajectory of the domestic and global economy attracted investors to longer-term tenors. The curve's rising short-term yields and falling longer-term yields largely tracked the yield curve movements of United States Treasuries, which were impacted by increased market expectations of less aggressive monetary tightening by the United States Federal Reserve.

In a surprise off-cycle move on 14 July, MAS decided to tighten its monetary policy again after increasing the slope and moving the center of its Singapore dollar nominal effective exchange rate policy band in April. In July, the central bank kept the slope unchanged but recentered the midpoint of the policy band to its prevailing level. This was the fourth consecutive tightening since October 2021, with the measure meant to temper inflationary pressure from increased commodity prices following the lifting of movement restrictions brought about by the coronavirus disease (COVID-19) pandemic. Global commodity and labor market constraints also contributed to inflationary pressure in Singapore.

Singapore's consumer price inflation has been on an uptrend since September 2021. In April, prices of basic goods and services increased 5.4% year-on-year (y-o-y), before accelerating to 5.6% y-o-y and 6.7% y-o-y in May and June, respectively. Consumer price inflation in July further surged to 7.0% y-o-y. During the first 7 months of 2022, the average inflation rate was 5.5% y-o-y, which fell within MAS's full-year 2022 inflation forecast of 5.0%–6.0%.

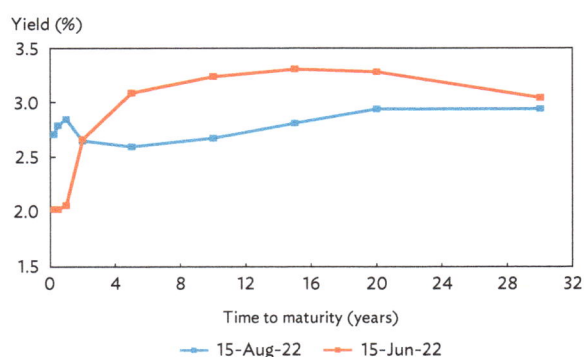

Figure 1: Singapore's Benchmark Yield Curve— Local Currency Government Bonds

Source: Based on data from Bloomberg LP.

The gross domestic product of Singapore increased 4.4% y-o-y in the second quarter (Q2) of 2022, accelerating from a 3.8% y-o-y expansion in the first quarter (Q1) of 2022. The growth was spurred by faster growth in the output of the manufacturing, construction, and services industries. On a quarter-on-quarter (q-o-q) basis, the economy of Singapore shrunk 0.2% in Q2 2022, reversing the jump of 0.8% q-o-q in the previous quarter. In August, the Ministry of Trade and Industry adjusted its projection of Singapore's 2022 annual economic growth to the 3.0%–4.0% range, narrower than its previous forecast of 3.0%–5.0%, as it expected weakening global economic developments to affect Singapore's economic performance.

Size and Composition

Singapore's LCY bond market grew 3.0% q-o-q in Q2 2022, reaching a size of SGD643.9 billion (USD463.1 billion) at the end of June and slightly decelerating from the 3.1% q-o-q growth in Q1 2022 (**Table 1**). On an annual basis, the LCY bond market expanded 17.3% y-o-y during Q2 2022, which was slower than the 20.9% y-o-y growth registered in the prior quarter. The growth in Singapore's LCY bond market was driven by growth in both the government and corporate bond segments, which accounted for 69.3% and 30.7%, respectively, of total LCY bonds outstanding at the end of June.

Table 1: Size and Composition of the Local Currency Bond Market in Singapore

| | Outstanding Amount (billion) | | | | | | Growth Rate (%) | | | |
| | Q2 2021 | | Q1 2022 | | Q2 2022 | | Q2 2021 | | Q2 2022 | |
	SGD	USD	SGD	USD	SGD	USD	q-o-q	y-o-y	q-o-q	y-o-y
Total	549	408	625	461	644	463	6.2	16.3	3.0	17.3
Government	366	272	430	318	446	321	4.8	19.7	3.8	22.0
SGS Bills and Bonds	207	154	222	164	226	163	1.7	6.2	2.0	9.5
MAS Bills	159	118	208	154	220	158	9.0	43.3	5.7	38.3
Corporate	183	136	195	144	198	142	9.3	10.0	1.4	7.9

( ) = negative, MAS = Monetary Authority of Singapore, q-o-q = quarter-on-quarter, Q1 = first quarter, Q2 = second quarter, SGD = Singapore dollar, SGS = Singapore Government Securities, USD = United States dollar, y-o-y = year-on-year.
Notes:
1. Corporate bonds are based on *AsianBondsOnline* estimates.
2. SGS bills and bonds do not include the special issue of SGS held by the Singapore Central Provident Fund.
3. Bloomberg LP end-of-period local currency–USD rates are used.
4. Growth rates are calculated from local currency base and do not include currency effects.
Sources: Bloomberg LP, Monetary Authority of Singapore, and Singapore Government Securities.

Issuance of LCY bonds in Q2 2022 jumped 16.1% q-o-q to SGD337.3 billion as issuances of both government and corporate bonds increased, reversing the contraction of 11.7% q-o-q recorded in Q1 2022.

Government bonds. LCY government bonds outstanding expanded 3.8% q-o-q in Q2 2022 to reach SGD446.4 billion at the end of June, slowing from the 4.5% q-o-q expansion logged in the previous quarter. Outstanding Singapore Government Securities bills and bonds, which comprised 50.7% of total LCY government bonds outstanding at the end of June, increased 2.0% q-o-q. MAS bills, which comprised the other 49.3%, jumped 5.7% q-o-q.

LCY government bond issuance increased 15.2% q-o-q in Q2 2022. Central bank bills issued during the quarter grew 14.6% q-o-q. The amount of Treasury securities issued during the quarter increased 20.1% q-o-q.

Corporate bonds. LCY corporate bonds outstanding increased 1.4% q-o-q in Q2 2022 to reach SGD197.5 billion at the end of June. This followed a marginal contraction registered in Q1 2022.

At the end of June, the top 30 issuers of LCY corporate bonds in Singapore had total bonds outstanding of SGD106.2 billion, or 53.8% of the LCY corporate bond market (**Table 2**). Government-owned Housing & Development Board was the largest

issuer in Q2 2022 with outstanding LCY corporate bonds totaling SGD27.0 billion. By sector, the largest share comprised real estate companies (39.4%) with SGD41.8 billion of total outstanding LCY corporate bonds at the end of June.

The issuance of LCY corporate bonds more than doubled in Q2 2022 to SGD5.2 billion from SGD2.4 billion in Q1 2022 as companies rushed to the debt market due to expectations of more interest rate hikes in the short term. The jump in issuance of LCY corporate bonds halted the trend of declining issuances that began in the third quarter of 2021.

In Q2 2022, state-owned Housing & Development Board raised SGD900.0 million worth of 3-year bonds with a coupon rate of 2.627% (**Table 3**). It was the largest LCY corporate issuance in Singapore in Q2 2022, the proceeds of which will be used for the company's development programs and general corporate purposes. Four companies in Singapore issued perpetual bonds drawn from their respective debt issuance programs during the quarter. The callable and floating-rate perpetual bond issuances ranged from SGD150.0 million to SGD500.0 million. Toward the end of April, real estate company Perennial Holdings sold a 2-year bond worth USD33.5 million and with a periodic distribution rate of 5.6%. This was the highest coupon rate of any LCY corporate bond issuance in Singapore during the review period.

Table 2: Top 30 Issuers of Local Currency Corporate Bonds in Singapore

	Issuers	Outstanding Amount		State-Owned	Listed Company	Type of Industry
		LCY Bonds (SGD billion)	LCY Bonds (USD billion)			
1.	Housing & Development Board	27.0	19.4	Yes	No	Real Estate
2.	Singapore Airlines	14.7	10.6	Yes	Yes	Transportation
3.	Land Transport Authority	9.5	6.8	Yes	No	Transportation
4.	Temasek Financial	5.1	3.7	Yes	No	Finance
5.	CapitaLand	4.6	3.3	Yes	Yes	Real Estate
6.	Sembcorp Industries	4.1	3.0	No	Yes	Diversified
7.	United Overseas Bank	4.0	2.9	No	Yes	Banking
8.	Frasers Property	3.3	2.4	No	Yes	Real Estate
9.	Mapletree Treasury Services	3.3	2.4	No	No	Finance
10.	DBS Bank	2.9	2.1	No	Yes	Banking
11.	Oversea-Chinese Banking Corporation	2.2	1.6	No	Yes	Banking
12.	Keppel Corporation	2.2	1.5	No	Yes	Diversified
13.	City Developments Limited	2.1	1.5	No	Yes	Real Estate
14.	CapitaLand Mall Trust	2.0	1.4	No	No	Finance
15.	Singapore Technologies Telemedia	1.7	1.2	Yes	No	Utilities
16.	National Environment Agency	1.7	1.2	Yes	No	Environmental Services
17.	Shangri-La Hotel	1.5	1.1	No	Yes	Real Estate
18.	NTUC Income	1.4	1.0	No	No	Finance
19.	Ascendas Real Estate Investment Trust	1.3	0.9	No	Yes	Finance
20.	PSA Treasury	1.3	0.9	Yes	No	Transportation
21.	Singtel Group Treasury	1.3	0.9	No	No	Finance
22.	Ascott Residence	1.2	0.8	No	Yes	Real Estate
23.	Suntec Real Estate Investment Trust	1.1	0.8	No	Yes	Real Estate
24.	Olam International	1.1	0.8	No	Yes	Consumer Goods
25.	GuocoLand Limited IHT	1.1	0.8	No	No	Real Estate
26.	Keppel Infrastructure Trust	1.1	0.8	No	No	Diversified
27.	Public Utilities Board	1.0	0.7	Yes	No	Utilities
28.	Singapore Post	1.0	0.7	No	Yes	Transportation
29.	Singapore Press Holdings	1.0	0.7	No	Yes	Communications
30.	StarHub	0.9	0.7	No	Yes	Diversified
	Total Top 30 LCY Corporate Issuers	**106.2**	**76.4**			
	Total LCY Corporate Bonds	**197.5**	**142.0**			
	Top 30 as % of Total LCY Corporate Bonds	**53.8%**	**53.8%**			

LCY = local currency, SGD = Singapore dollar, USD = United States dollar.
Notes:
1. Data as of 30 June 2022.
2. State-owned firms are defined as those in which the government has more than a 50% ownership stake.
Source: *AsianBondsOnline* calculations based on Bloomberg LP data.

Table 3: Notable Local Currency Corporate Bond Issuances in the Second Quarter of 2022

Corporate Issuers	Coupon Rate (%)	Issued Amount (SGD million)
Housing & Development Board		
3-year bond	2.627	900.0
Oversea-Chinese Banking Corporation		
Perpetual bond	3.900	500.0
Singapore Post		
Perpetual bond	4.350	250.0
Lendlease Global Commercial REIT		
Perpetual bond	5.250	200.0
ESR-LOGOS REIT		
Perpetual bond	5.500	150.0
Perennial Holdings		
2-year bond	5.600	33.5

REIT = real estate investment trust, SGD = Singapore dollar.
Source: Bloomberg LP.

Policy, Institutional, and Regulatory Developments

Singapore Green Bond Framework Launched

On 9 June, the Government of Singapore published its Singapore Green Bond Framework, which provides guidelines for issuances of sovereign green bonds under the government's Significant Infrastructure Government Loan Act. The framework adheres to international best practices, outlining recognized market standards, strict oversight of the selection of projects and allocation of proceeds, and evaluation of green projects. The framework also stipulates that proceeds from green bonds issued by government agencies will be used to finance green projects under the Singapore Green Plan 2030, which facilitates the economy's transition to a low-carbon economy and advances the United Nation's Sustainable Development Goals.

Singapore Prices First Sovereign Green Bond

On 4 August, MAS priced its first sovereign green bond, known as the Green Singapore Government Securities Bond. The issuance was a 50-year bond worth SGD2.4 billion with a coupon rate of 3.0%. The 50-year tenor is the longest-dated green bond ever issued by the Government of Singapore. The bond also supports Singapore's goal of being a low-carbon economy and a green finance hub. Extending Singapore's bond yield curve also helps the development of the Singapore dollar bond market.

Thailand

Yield Movements

Between 15 June and 15 August, Thailand's local currency (LCY) government bond yield curve flattened, with yields rising at the shorter-end but falling along the rest of the curve (**Figure 1**). Yields for tenors below 2 years gained 8 basis points (bps) on average, while yields for bonds with maturities of 2 years or longer fell an average of 58 bps. The 6-month bond posted the largest yield gain at 17 bps, while the 6-year bond recorded the sharpest yield drop at 78 bps. The 2-year bond yield shed 29 bps, while the 10-year bond yield fell 64 bps. As a result, the spread of the 10-year yield over the 2-year yield narrowed from 117 bps on 15 June to 82 bps on 15 August.

Yields rose at the shorter-end of the curve in response to monetary policy tightening by the Bank of Thailand (BOT). On 10 August, the BOT raised its benchmark policy rate by 25 bps to 0.75% and signaled that monetary policy normalization would be gradual. The BOT was among the last of the region's central banks to start monetary policy normalization. A better-than-expected economic performance in the second quarter (Q2) of 2022, along with elevated inflation, prompted the pivot to policy tightening.

Thailand's inflation remained among the highest in the region. Consumer price inflation rose to 7.9% year-on-year (y-o-y) in August from 7.6% y-o-y in July and 7.7% y-o-y in June. High global energy prices continued to be the main source of inflationary pressure. The BOT expects inflation to remain elevated for the rest of 2022, but then to gradually fall within the target range of 1.0%–3.0% in 2023 as supply-side inflationary pressure subsides.

Medium- to long-term inflation expectations remain anchored within the BOT target range and contributed to the decline in yields for bonds with maturities of 2 years or longer. Improved market sentiment also revived demand for bonds, raising prices and lowering yields. Global financial conditions generally improved at the end of July, after the United States (US) Federal Reserve announced an expected rate hike of 75 bps and indicated that the pace of monetary policy tightening would decelerate.

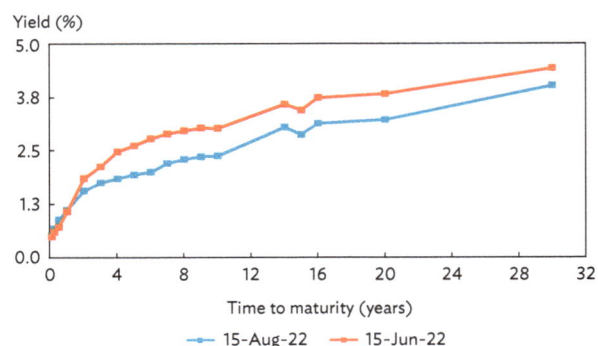

Figure 1: Thailand's Benchmark Yield Curve— Local Currency Government Bonds

Sources: Based on data from Bloomberg LP.

Domestic financial conditions were also buoyed by the sustained economic recovery. Thailand's economy continued to gain pace, with gross domestic product (GDP) growth rising to 2.5% y-o-y in Q2 2022 from 2.3% y-o-y in the previous quarter, driven primarily by a revival of tourism. Thailand began progressively relaxing quarantine requirements and testing protocols for travelers in May. As a result, the number of foreign tourist arrivals more than tripled to 1.6 million in Q2 2022 from 0.5 million in the prior quarter. Private consumption rose 6.9% y-o-y in Q2 2022 as economic activities continued to normalize. Government consumption rose 2.4% y-o-y, while exports expanded 8.5% y-o-y. In August, the National Economic and Social Development Council revised its GDP growth forecast for full-year 2022 to 2.7%–3.2% from the June projection of 2.5%–3.5%.

Size and Composition

Thailand's LCY bond market reached a size of THB15,107.8 billion (USD427.3 billion) at the end of June (**Table 1**). Overall growth eased to 0.7% quarter-on-quarter (q-o-q) and 6.4% y-o-y in Q2 2022 from 1.8% q-o-q and 8.4% y-o-y in the first quarter (Q1) of 2022. The growth slowdown was mainly due to a contraction in the government bond segment, which outpaced the expansion in the corporate bond segment.

Table 1: Size and Composition of the Local Currency Bond Market in Thailand

	Outstanding Amount (billion)						Growth Rate (%)			
	Q2 2021		Q1 2022		Q2 2022		Q2 2021		Q2 2022	
	THB	USD	THB	USD	THB	USD	q-o-q	y-o-y	q-o-q	y-o-y
Total	14,203	443	14,998	451	15,108	427	2.6	5.6	0.7	6.4
Government	10,324	322	10,937	329	10,860	307	1.7	6.1	(0.7)	5.2
Government Bonds and Treasury Bills	6,485	202	7,163	215	7,327	207	2.1	22.2	2.3	13.0
Central Bank Bonds	2,917	91	2,822	85	2,571	73	0.2	(19.7)	(8.9)	(11.9)
State-Owned Enterprise and Other Bonds	921	29	953	29	962	27	3.2	16.2	1.0	4.5
Corporate	3,880	121	4,061	122	4,247	120	5.1	4.4	4.6	9.5

( ) = negative, q-o-q = quarter-on-quarter, Q1 = first quarter, Q2 = second quarter, THB = Thai baht, USD = United States dollar, y-o-y = year-on-year.
Notes:
1. Bloomberg LP end-of-period local currency–USD rates are used.
2. Growth rates are calculated from local currency base and do not include currency effects.
Source: Bank of Thailand.

Government bonds continued to dominate Thailand's LCY bond market. At the end of June, government bonds comprised 71.9% of total bonds outstanding, while corporate bonds represented the remaining 28.1%.

Government bonds. LCY government bonds outstanding amounted to THB10,860.5 billion at the end of June. The LCY government bond market contracted 0.7% q-o-q in Q2 2022, reversing the 2.1% q-o-q growth in the prior quarter. The decline was driven by a drop in BOT bonds, which outpaced growth in government bonds and Treasury bills, and in state-owned enterprise and other bonds. The stock of BOT bonds contracted 8.9% q-o-q in Q2 2022 due to maturities and a drop in issuance. Meanwhile, growth in outstanding government bonds and Treasury bills eased to 2.3% q-o-q in Q2 2022 from 4.1% q-o-q in the previous quarter. The outstanding stock of state-owned enterprise and other bonds continued to post modest growth, rising 1.0% q-o-q in Q2 2022 after a 1.8% q-o-q rise in the preceding quarter. On an annual basis, growth in Thailand's LCY government bond market eased to 5.2% y-o-y in Q2 2022 from 7.7% y-o-y in Q1 2022.

Government bonds and Treasury bills continued to account for the largest share of LCY government bonds. Outstanding government bonds and Treasury bills totaled THB7,327.3 billion at the end of June, comprising 67.5% of the LCY government bond market. BOT bonds (THB2,571.1 billion) and state-owned enterprise and other bonds (THB962.1 billion) accounted for 23.7% and 8.9%, respectively, of total government bonds outstanding at the end of June.

Issuance of new LCY government bonds amounted to THB1,571.9 billion in Q2 2022. Issuance continued to decline, dropping 5.9% q-o-q in Q2 2022 after a 0.4% q-o-q dip in the previous quarter, as the government tapered borrowing amid continued economic recovery. Issuance of government bonds and Treasury bills rose 22.9% q-o-q in Q2 2022, driven largely by a record-high issuance of retails savings bonds in June. The government raised a total of THB52.7 billion from five tranches of retail savings bonds dubbed as "Happy Savings," which were issued to individuals and nonprofit organizations. The Public Debt Management Office (PDMO) opted to tap retail investors to avoid an oversupply of bonds in the institutional market and to develop a savings alternative for bank deposits. The issuance of state-owned enterprise and other bonds rebounded, rising 101.8% q-o-q in Q2 2022 after a 35.2% q-o-q drop in the previous quarter. Meanwhile, BOT bond issuance contracted 21.8% q-o-q, due in part to reduced issuance of 2-year BOT bonds to accommodate the PDMO's issuance of bonds with tenors of 3–5 years.

On a y-o-y basis, government bond issuance contracted further by 9.1% in Q2 2022, after declining 1.0% in Q1 2022, as the government eased borrowings to manage fiscal sustainability. The share of public debt to GDP inched up to 60.9% at the end of June from 60.6% at the end of March.

Corporate bonds. Thailand's LCY corporate bond market reached a size of THB4,247.3 billion at the end of June. Growth jumped to 4.6% q-o-q in Q2 2022 from 1.2% q-o-q in the previous quarter on the back of robust issuance as the sustained economic recovery boosted investor confidence. On a y-o-y basis, growth in outstanding LCY corporate bonds eased to 9.5% in Q2 2022 from 10.1% in Q1 2022.

At the end of June, the LCY bonds outstanding of the top 30 corporate issuers in Thailand totaled THB2,441.6 billion, representing 57.5% of the Thai LCY corporate bond market (**Table 2**). The top 30

Table 2: Top 30 Issuers of Local Currency Corporate Bonds in Thailand

	Issuers	Outstanding Amount		State-Owned	Listed Company	Type of Industry
		LCY Bonds (THB billion)	LCY Bonds (USD billion)			
1.	CP ALL	246.5	7.0	No	Yes	Commerce
2.	True Corporation	172.8	4.9	No	Yes	Communications
3.	PTT	160.4	4.5	Yes	Yes	Energy and Utilities
4.	Siam Cement	135.0	3.8	Yes	Yes	Construction Material
5.	Thai Beverage	129.2	3.7	No	No	Food and Beverage
6.	Charoen Pokphand Foods	123.6	3.5	No	Yes	Food and Beverage
7.	Berli Jucker	107.4	3.0	No	Yes	Commerce
8.	True Move H Universal Communication	93.2	2.6	No	No	Communications
9.	CPF Thailand	89.2	2.5	No	No	Food and Beverage
10.	PTT Global Chemical	86.7	2.5	No	Yes	Petrochemicals and Chemicals
11.	Indorama Ventures	80.6	2.3	No	Yes	Petrochemicals and Chemicals
12.	Bank of Ayudhya	79.9	2.3	No	Yes	Banking
13.	Banpu	70.3	2.0	No	Yes	Energy and Utilities
14.	Gulf Energy Development	69.5	2.0	No	Yes	Energy and Utilities
15.	Bangkok Commercial Asset Management	68.3	1.9	No	Yes	Finance and Securities
16.	Minor International	67.1	1.9	No	Yes	Hospitality and Leisure
17.	Krung Thai Bank	62.1	1.8	Yes	Yes	Banking
18.	Toyota Leasing Thailand	60.4	1.7	No	No	Finance and Securities
19.	Muangthai Capital	58.0	1.6	No	Yes	Finance and Securities
20.	BTS Group Holdings	54.8	1.5	No	Yes	Transportation and Logistics
21.	Global Power Synergy	53.5	1.5	No	Yes	Energy and Utilities
22.	TPI Polene	46.5	1.3	No	Yes	Property and Construction
23.	dtac TriNet	43.5	1.2	No	Yes	Communications
24.	Magnolia Quality Development	43.2	1.2	No	No	Real Estate
25.	Krungthai Card	42.5	1.2	No	Yes	Finance and Securities
26.	B.Grimm Power	40.7	1.2	No	Yes	Energy and Utilities
27.	Sansiri	40.2	1.1	No	Yes	Property and Construction
28.	CH. Karnchang	39.9	1.1	No	Yes	Property and Construction
29.	Bangkok Expressway & Metro	39.1	1.1	No	Yes	Transportation and Logistics
30.	ICBC Thai Leasing	37.8	1.1	No	No	Finance and Securities
	Total Top 30 LCY Corporate Issuers	**2,441.6**	**69.1**			
	Total LCY Corporate Bonds	**4,247.3**	**120.1**			
	Top 30 as % of Total LCY Corporate Bonds	**57.5%**	**57.5%**			

LCY = local currency, THB = Thai baht, USD = United States dollar.
Notes:
1. Data as of 30 June 2022.
2. State-owned firms are defined as those in which the government has more than a 50% ownership stake.
Source: *AsianBondsOnline* calculations based on Bloomberg LP data.

issuers were predominantly companies in the energy and utilities, commerce, and food and beverage sectors. A majority of the top 30 were listed on the Stock Exchange of Thailand and only three were state-owned. CP ALL continued to top the list with an outstanding bond stock of THB246.5 billion. The next largest issuers were True Corporation, PTT, Siam Cement, and Thai Beverage—with outstanding bond stocks of THB172.8 billion, THB160.4 billion, THB135.0 billion, and THB129.2 billion, respectively.

Corporate debt issuance in Q2 2022 totaled THB597.3 billion. Growth accelerated to 36.3% q-o-q in Q2 2022 from 19.5% q-o-q in the prior quarter as corporates locked in low borrowing rates. The BOT held its benchmark policy rate at a record low of 0.50% for most of the review period before raising the rate by 25 bps on 10 August. Corporate borrowings also rose on the back of improved market sentiment as the economic recovery accelerated with the revival of tourism. On a y-o-y basis, corporate debt issuance rose 25.1% in Q2 2022, following a 48.6% jump in the preceding quarter.

A total of 94 companies tapped the bond market for their financing needs in Q2 2022. Notable issuers in Q2 2022 are listed in **Table 3**. PTT, SCG Chemicals, and PTT Global Chemical were the top issuers during the quarter—with total issuances of THB40.0 billion, THB30.0 billion, and THB25.0 billion, respectively. Global Power Synergy raised a total of THB12.0 billion from a five-tranche issuance of green bonds with maturities ranging from 3 years to 15 years and coupon rates ranging from 2.55% to 4.40%. Proceeds from the issuance will be used for renewable energy projects. B.Grimm Power, an energy company, also issued two green bonds during the quarter: a 3-year bond carrying a coupon of 2.86% worth THB0.3 billion and a 5-year bond carrying a coupon of 3.79% worth THB3.0 billion.

Investor Profiles

Central government bonds. Financial corporations, other depository corporations, the central government, and nonresidents remained the primary holders of government bonds at the end of June 2022 (**Figure 2**). Financial corporations continued to hold over a third of total government bonds, although their share slid to 36.3% at the end of June 2022 from 38.9% a year earlier. Other depository corporations, which include commercial banks and finance companies, were the second-largest

Table 3: Notable Local Currency Corporate Bond Issuances in the Second Quarter of 2022

Corporate Issuers	Coupon Rate (%)	Issued Amount (THB billion)
PTT		
3-year bond	1.79	8.0
5.5-year bond	2.45	3.0
7-year bond	3.25	20.0
12-year bond	3.47	9.0
SCG Chemicals		
4-year bond	2.75	30.0
PTT Global Chemical		
5-year bond	3.21	5.0
7-year bond	3.50	17.0
12-year bond	4.00	3.0
UOB Thai		
2-year bond	1.53	2.5
3-year bond	2.01	2.5
10-year bond	4.07	13.7
Krung Thai Bank		
10-year bond	3.25	18.1
B.Grimm Power[a]		
3-year bond	2.91	4.2
3-year bond[b]	2.86	0.3
5-year bond[b]	3.79	3.0
7-year bond	4.15	2.2
10-year bond	4.53	2.6
Global Power Synergy		
3-year bond[b]	2.55	1.0
5-year bond[b]	3.04	3.0
8-year bond[b]	3.56	1.0
10-year bond[b]	3.75	3.0
15-year bond[b]	4.40	4.0

THB = Thai baht.
[a] Multiple issuance of the same tenor indicates issuance on different dates.
[b] Green bonds.
Source: Bloomberg LP.

holder of government bonds with a share of 23.2% at the end of June 2022. The central government, including state-owned nonprofit enterprises and the Social Security Office, had a 14.7% share at the end of June 2022. Nonresidents' share of government bonds slipped to 13.2% in June 2022 from 13.7% in June 2021.

Central bank bonds. At the end of June 2022, the primary holders of BOT bonds were other depository corporations and financial corporations (**Figure 3**). The share of other depository corporations rose to 42.5% in June 2022 from 37.8% in June 2021, while financial corporations' holdings slid to 31.2% from 33.9% during the same period. The BOT's holdings of its own LCY bonds dropped to 11.2% at the end of June from 14.6% a year earlier. Nonresidents' holdings of central bank bonds rose to 2.3% at the end of June 2022 from 0.7% a year earlier.

Figure 2: Local Currency Government Bonds Investor Profile

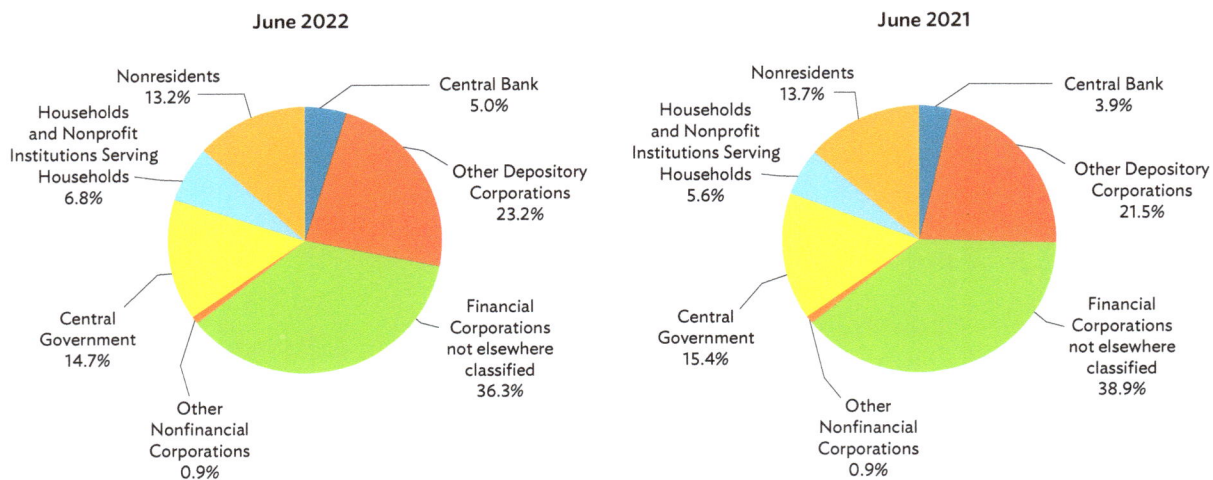

June 2022

Nonresidents 13.2%
Central Bank 5.0%
Households and Nonprofit Institutions Serving Households 6.8%
Other Depository Corporations 23.2%
Central Government 14.7%
Financial Corporations not elsewhere classified 36.3%
Other Nonfinancial Corporations 0.9%

June 2021

Nonresidents 13.7%
Central Bank 3.9%
Households and Nonprofit Institutions Serving Households 5.6%
Other Depository Corporations 21.5%
Central Government 15.4%
Financial Corporations not elsewhere classified 38.9%
Other Nonfinancial Corporations 0.9%

Note: Government bonds include Treasury bills and bonds.
Source: AsianBondsOnline and Bank of Thailand.

Figure 3: Local Currency Central Bank Securities Investor Profile

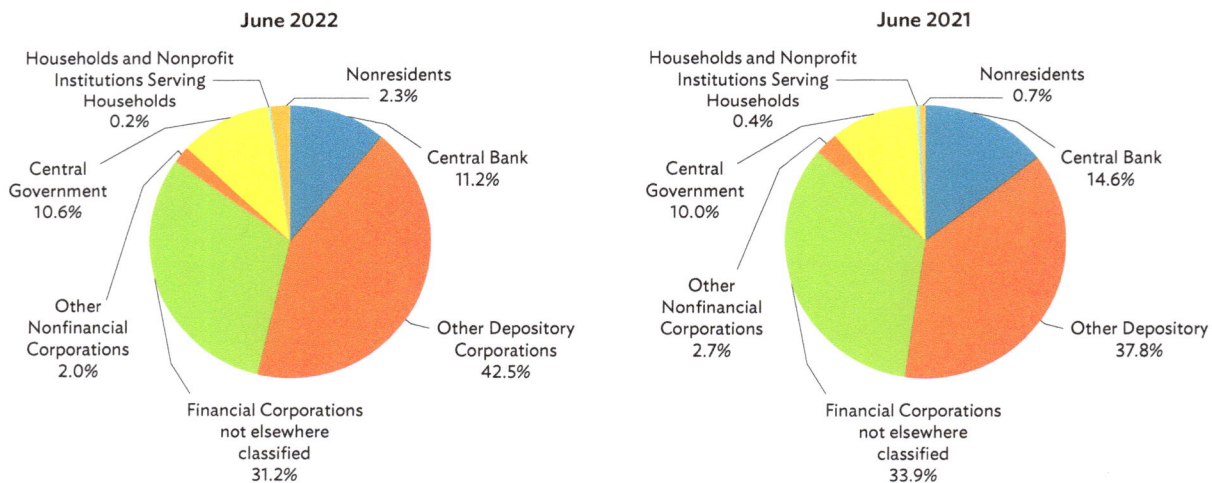

June 2022

Households and Nonprofit Institutions Serving Households 0.2%
Nonresidents 2.3%
Central Bank 11.2%
Central Government 10.6%
Other Depository Corporations 42.5%
Other Nonfinancial Corporations 2.0%
Financial Corporations not elsewhere classified 31.2%

June 2021

Households and Nonprofit Institutions Serving Households 0.4%
Nonresidents 0.7%
Central Bank 14.6%
Central Government 10.0%
Other Depository 37.8%
Other Nonfinancial Corporations 2.7%
Financial Corporations not elsewhere classified 33.9%

Source: Bank of Thailand.

The Thai LCY bond market recorded net inflows from foreign investors of THB22.2 billion in Q2 2022 (**Figure 4**). April and May saw net inflows of THB7.6 billion and THB30.0 billion, respectively, as the gradual removal of pandemic-induced movement restrictions and the return of tourists revived market sentiment. In June and July, the US Federal Reserve's consecutive rate hikes widened the rate differentials between the US Treasury and Thai sovereign rates, resulting in net outflows from the Thai bond market.

Figure 4: Foreign Investor Net Trading of Local Currency Bonds in Thailand

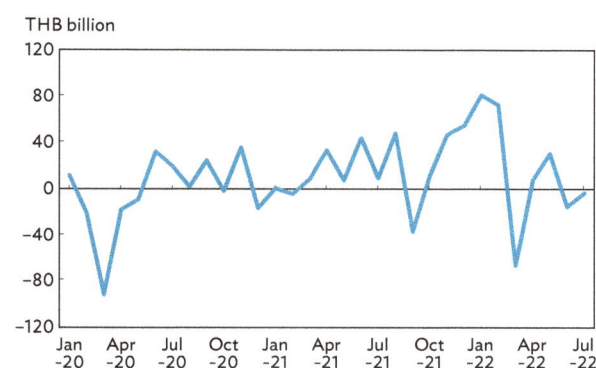

THB = Thai baht.
Source: Thai Bond Market Association.

Ratings Update

On 21 June, Fitch Ratings affirmed Thailand's long-term foreign currency default rating at BBB+ with a stable outlook. The rating affirmation was supported by Thailand's robust external position and strong macroeconomic policy framework. The ratings agency viewed that Thailand's resilient external finances provide ample buffer to withstand tightening global financial conditions and rising geopolitical risks. Fitch Ratings expects Thailand's GDP to rise 3.2% in 2022 and 4.5% in 2023.

Policy, Institutional, and Regulatory Developments

Public Debt Management Office Announces Results of Bond-Switching Transactions

On 13 May, the PDMO announced the results of bond-switching transactions for government bonds totaling THB90.0 billion. The bond swap allowed bond holders to switch bonds with shorter maturities for those with longer maturities. The bond swap involved five source bonds with remaining maturities ranging from 0.6 year to 2.6 years and 10 destination bonds with remaining maturities ranging from 4.6 years to 50.1 years. Bond swap operations provide bond holders with an opportunity to adjust their investment portfolio and allow the government to extend its debt maturity profile, thereby reducing debt redemption pressures and boosting liquidity.

Viet Nam

Yield Movements

Local currency (LCY) government bond yields in Viet Nam rose for all tenors between 15 June and 15 August, leading the entire yield curve to shift upward (**Figure 1**). Bond yields for maturities of 3 years or less climbed the most, rising an average of 81 basis points (bps), while yields for maturities of 5 years or more gained an average of 23 bps during the review period. The yield curve flattened as yields at the shorter-end rose at a faster pace, causing the spread between the 10-year over 2-year tenors to narrow from 121 bps on 15 June to 54 bps on 15 August.

Bond yield movements in Viet Nam bucked the regional trend as it was the sole market in emerging East Asia where yields rose across the curve. The rise in yields was largely influenced by the State Bank of Vietnam (SBV) opting to utilize open market operations to manage the money supply and stabilize the exchange rate. The SBV is aiming to keep interbank rates elevated by setting an interest rate floor in its open market operations to maintain a spread between VND-denominated loans and USD-denominated loans. This move also indirectly contributed to the uptick in yields across the curve. In recent months, the central bank has resumed issuance of central bank bills and limited credit growth quotas for banks, withdrawing liquidity from the market.

The uptick in yields was also partly driven by Viet Nam's strong economic performance in the second quarter (Q2) of 2022. Real gross domestic product (GDP) growth climbed to 7.7% year-on-year (y-o-y) in Q2 2022 from 5.0% y-o-y in the first quarter (Q1) of 2022, the fastest pace to-date and higher than the government's full-year target. Economic growth was underpinned by the recovery in exports and growth across all industry sectors. Amid the strong GDP growth, the Ministry of Planning and Investment revised upward the 2022 growth target to 7.0% from 6.0%–6.5%.

The SBV has yet to raise policy rate unlike its peers in emerging East Asia, preferring to utilize open market operations to achieve its goals. Consumer price inflation has been relatively tame compared with that of other regional markets. Although inflation has been inching up

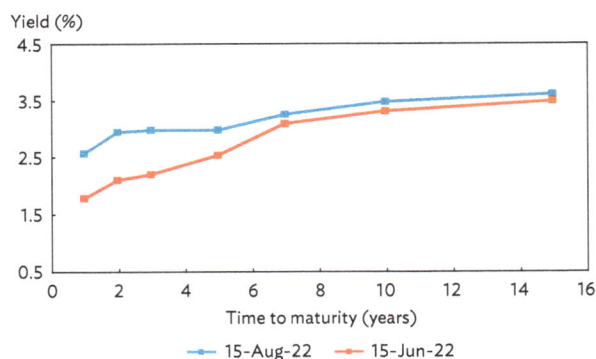

Figure 1: Viet Nam's Benchmark Yield Curve— Local Currency Government Bonds

Source: Based on data from Bloomberg LP.

in recent months, it has remained below the government's limit of 4.0% for 2022. Consumer price inflation eased from 3.4% y-o-y in June to 3.1% y-o-y in July and 2.9% y-o-y in August. The government is confident that inflation will not exceed 4.0% this year.

Size and Composition

The LCY bond market's growth soared to 8.1% quarter-on-quarter (q-o-q) to reach a size of VND2,315.9 trillion (USD99.5 billion) at the end of June. Growth was faster than the 2.4% q-o-q expansion in the prior quarter (**Table 1**). The faster growth was contributed by both the government and corporate bond segments. Relative to the same quarter in the previous year, the bond market expanded 31.6% y-o-y in Q2 2022, up from the 29.2% y-o-y expansion in Q1 2022. The LCY bond market remained dominated by government bonds, which accounted for 70.2% share of the total bond stock at the end of June. The remaining 29.8% share was accounted for by corporate bonds whose share inched up from 29.4% in Q1 2022.

Government bonds. The outstanding size of Viet Nam's LCY government bond market reached VND1,626.2 trillion at the end of June on growth of 7.4% q-o-q. Much of the growth was contributed by central bank bills, which grew substantially during the review period.

Table 1: Size and Composition of the Local Currency Bond Market in Viet Nam

| | Outstanding Amount (billion) | | | | | | Growth Rate (%) | | | |
| | Q2 2021 | | Q1 2022 | | Q2 2022 | | Q2 2021 | | Q2 2022 | |
	VND	USD	VND	USD	VND	USD	q-o-q	y-o-y	q-o-q	y-o-y
Total	1,759,977	76	2,143,134	94	2,315,918	99	6.1	27.6	8.1	31.6
Government	1,357,573	59	1,513,514	66	1,626,199	70	(0.5)	14.7	7.4	19.8
Treasury Bonds	1,221,237	53	1,373,782	60	1,385,244	59	0.1	17.5	0.8	13.4
Central Bank Bills	0	0	4,387	0	102,410	4	–	–	2,234.6	–
Government-Guaranteed and Municipal Bonds	136,337	6	135,346	6	138,546	6	(5.3)	(5.3)	2.4	1.6
Corporate	402,404	17	629,620	28	689,719	30	36.4	105.1	9.5	71.4

( ) = negative, – = not applicable, q-o-q = quarter-on-quarter, Q1 = first quarter, Q2 = second quarter, USD = United States dollar, VND = Vietnamese dong, y-o-y = year-on-year.
Notes:
1. Bloomberg LP end-of-period local currency–USD rates are used.
2. Growth rates are calculated from local currency base and do not include currency effects.
Sources: Bloomberg LP and Vietnam Bond Market Association.

Treasury bonds continued to account for a majority of government bonds in Viet Nam at a size of VND1,385.2 trillion. Growth, however, was marginal at 0.8% q-o-q in Q2 2022 versus 1.8% q-o-q in Q1 2022. The aggressive monetary policy action of the United States Federal Reserve acted as a drag on growth in most regional bond markets, resulting in the weakening of global financial conditions. This led to a decline in issuance in Viet Nam in Q2 2022, as investors sought higher returns. Issuance of Treasury bonds totaled VND27.8 trillion on a decline of 32.6% q-o-q in Q2 2022.

Government-guaranteed bonds, which accounted for 8.5% of the government bond total at the end of June, posted modest growth of 2.4%, a reversal from the 4.5% q-o-q contraction at the end of March. The increase in the bond stock was driven by the issuances of the Vietnam Bank for Social Policies, which issued several times each month during the quarter, totaling VND5.0 trillion.

Central bank bills posted the fastest growth among all bond segments, as robust issuance during the quarter lifted the central bank bond stock to VND102.4 trillion at the end of June from VND4.4 trillion at the end of March. The central bank has actively engaged in open market operations to manage liquidity conditions and the exchange rate. Amid the Federal Reserve's aggressive tightening, the SBV continued to issue bills to help stabilize the VND–USD exchange rate. Issuance of central bank bills during the quarter surged to VND167.7 trillion in Q2 2022 from only VND31.7 trillion in Q1 2022. SBV bill issuance during the quarter accounted for 83.6% of Viet Nam's government bond issuance total in Q2 2022.

Corporate bonds. At the end of June, the corporate bond stock climbed to VND689.7 trillion on growth of 9.5% q-o-q. Growth quickened from only 4.6% q-o-q at the end of March. The faster growth in outstanding corporate bonds was fueled by hefty issuance volume during the quarter, which totaled VND69.1 trillion for a 120.5% q-o-q hike, on renewed optimism as economic activities normalized and domestic economic growth outpaced expectations.

At the end of June, the outstanding bond stock of Viet Nam's top 30 corporate issuers totaled VND414.7 trillion, comprising 60.1% of the LCY corporate bond market (**Table 2**). Viet Nam's top corporate bond issuers were predominantly banks and property firms, which collectively held 55.5% of the total LCY corporate bonds outstanding at the end of June. State-owned Bank for Investment and Development of Vietnam (BIDV) remained the top issuer, with an outstanding bond stock of VND53.4 trillion at the end of June. BIDV accounted for 7.7% of the total corporate bond stock of Viet Nam at the end of Q2 2022.

Corporate bond issuance in Q2 2022 totaled VND69.1 trillion, rebounding during the quarter to rise 120.5% q-o-q after a 74.6% q-o-q drop in the previous quarter, as the strong economic recovery boosted investor confidence. The largest corporate bond issuances in Q2 2022 are presented in **Table 3**. Leading the list were three banking institutions. State-owned BIDV had aggregate issuance amounting to VND12.5 trillion in multiple tranches. Next were Military Commercial Joint Stock Bank with bond issuance totaling VND9.8 trillion in

Table 2: Top 30 Issuers of Local Currency Corporate Bonds in Viet Nam

	Issuers	Outstanding Amount		State-Owned	Listed Company	Type of Industry
		LCY Bonds (VND billion)	LCY Bonds (USD billion)			
1.	Bank for Investment and Development of Vietnam	53,368	2.29	Yes	Yes	Banking
2.	Vietnam Prosperity Joint Stock Commercial Bank	29,250	1.26	No	Yes	Banking
3.	Vietnam International Joint Stock Commercial Bank	28,950	1.24	No	Yes	Banking
4.	Ho Chi Minh City Development Joint Stock Commercial Bank	24,998	1.07	No	Yes	Banking
5.	Asia Commercial Joint Stock Bank	24,900	1.07	No	Yes	Banking
6.	Lien Viet Post Joint Stock Commercial Bank	24,590	1.06	No	Yes	Banking
7.	Orient Commercial Joint Stock Bank	23,935	1.03	No	No	Banking
8.	Masan Group	18,300	0.79	No	Yes	Finance
9.	Tien Phong Commercial Joint Stock Bank	17,649	0.76	No	Yes	Banking
10.	Military Commercial Joint Stock Bank	15,046	0.65	No	Yes	Banking
11.	Vietnam Joint Stock Commercial Bank for Industry and Trade	13,689	0.59	Yes	Yes	Banking
12.	Vietnam Technological and Commercial Joint Stock Bank	13,600	0.58	No	Yes	Banking
13.	An Binh Commercial Joint Stock Bank	11,000	0.47	No	No	Banking
14.	NoVa Real Estate Investment Corporation JSC	10,981	0.47	No	Yes	Property
15.	Saigon - Ha Noi Commercial Joint Stock Bank	10,150	0.44	No	Yes	Banking
16.	Vietnam Maritime Joint Stock Commercial Bank	9,999	0.43	No	Yes	Banking
17.	Vinhomes JSC	9,935	0.43	No	Yes	Property
18.	Sovico Group Joint Stock Company	8,550	0.37	No	Yes	Property
19.	Saigon Glory Company Limited	8,000	0.34	No	No	Property
20.	Bac A Commercial Joint Stock Bank	7,300	0.31	No	Yes	Banking
21.	Southeast Asia Commercial Joint Stock Bank	7,076	0.30	No	Yes	Banking
22	Golden Hill Real Estate JSC	5,701	0.24	No	No	Property
23.	Vingroup	5,425	0.23	No	Yes	Property
24.	Mediterranean Revival Villas Company Limited	5,000	0.21	No	No	Property
25.	Bong Sen JSC	4,800	0.21	No	No	Manufacturing
26.	Thai Son–Long An JSC	4,600	0.20	No	No	Property
27.	Vietnam Bank for Agriculture and Rural Development	4,600	0.20	Yes	No	Banking
28.	Phu My Hung Corporation	4,497	0.19	No	No	Property
29.	Trung Nam Dak Lak 1 Wind Power JSC	4,400	0.19	No	No	Energy
30.	VPBank SMBC Finance Company Limited	4,400	0.19	No	No	Finance
	Total Top 30 LCY Corporate Issuers	**414,688**	**17.81**			
	Total LCY Corporate Bonds	**689,719**	**29.62**			
	Top 30 as % of Total LCY Corporate Bonds	**60.1%**	**60.1%**			

LCY = local currency, USD = United States dollar, VND = Vietnamese dong.
Notes:
1. Data as of 30 June 2022.
2. State-owned firms are defined as those in which the government has more than a 50% ownership stake.
Sources: *AsianBondsOnline* calculations based on Bloomberg LP and Vietnam Bond Market Association data.

Table 3: Notable Local Currency Corporate Bond Issuances in the Second Quarter of 2022

Corporate Issuers	Coupon Rate (%)	Issued Amount (VND billion)	Corporate Issuers	Coupon Rate (%)	Issued Amount (VND billion)
Bank for Investment and Development of Vietnam[a]			Military Commercial and Joint Stock Bank[a]		
1.25-year bond	3.80	2,300	3-year bond	4.00	2,500
1.25-year bond	3.80	1,700	3-year bond	–	2,000
2-year bond	4.20	1,000	3-year bond	–	1,300
8-year bond	0.9% + average interest rate for 12-month deposit	2,000	3-year bond	–	1,000
			3-year bond	–	700
8-year bond	0.9% + average interest rate for 12-month deposit	1,981	3-year bond	–	700
			3-year bond	–	200
8-year bond	0.9% + average interest rate for 12-month reference rate	1,150	5-year bond	–	50
			5-year bond	–	40
			5.27-year bond	1.4% + reference rate	50
8-year bond	0.9% + average interest rate for 12-month deposit	1,000	7-year bond	–	1,010
			7-year bond	–	100
8-year bond	0.9% + average interest rate for 12-month reference rate	500	7-year bond	1.3% + reference rate	100
			7-year bond	7.05	50
8-year bond	0.9% + average interest rate for 12-month deposit	460	7-year bond	1.3% + reference rate	30
10-year bond	1.3% + average interest rate for 12-month deposit	200	Vietnam Technological and Commercial Joint Stock Bank[a]		
			3-year bond	4.30	1,500
			3-year bond	4.20	1,500
10-year bond	1.0% + average interest rate for 12-month deposit	14	3-year bond	4.30	1,500
			3-year bond	–	1,000
15-year bond	0.9% + average interest rate for 12-month reference rate	200	3-year bond	4.20	1,000
			3-year bond	4.20	1,000
			3-year bond	4.20	500

– = not available, VND = Vietnamese dong.
[a] Multiple issuance of the same tenor indicates issuance on different dates.
Source: Vietnam Bond Market Association.

multiple issuances of 3-year, 5-year, and 7-year bonds and Vietnam Technological and Commercial Joint Stock Bank with issuances of VND8.0 trillion.

In Q2 2022, a total of 98 new corporate bonds were added to the corporate bond stock, with issuances coming from 38 corporate firms. The shortest-dated issuance for the quarter was a 1-year bond, while the longest was a 15-year bond. Most corporate bonds issued in Viet Nam carried floating-rate coupons. Most of the new bond issuances came from the banking sector.

Investor Profile

Insurance companies and banks continued to hold the majority of LCY government bonds in Viet Nam (**Figure 2**). Insurance companies' share of total government bonds outstanding rose to 58.8% at the end of June 2022 from 57.1% a year earlier. During the same period, banks' holdings of government bonds slipped to 40.5% from 42.0%. Foreign holdings of government bonds remained minimal at less than 1.0% at the end of June.

Figure 2: Local Currency Government Bonds Investor Profile

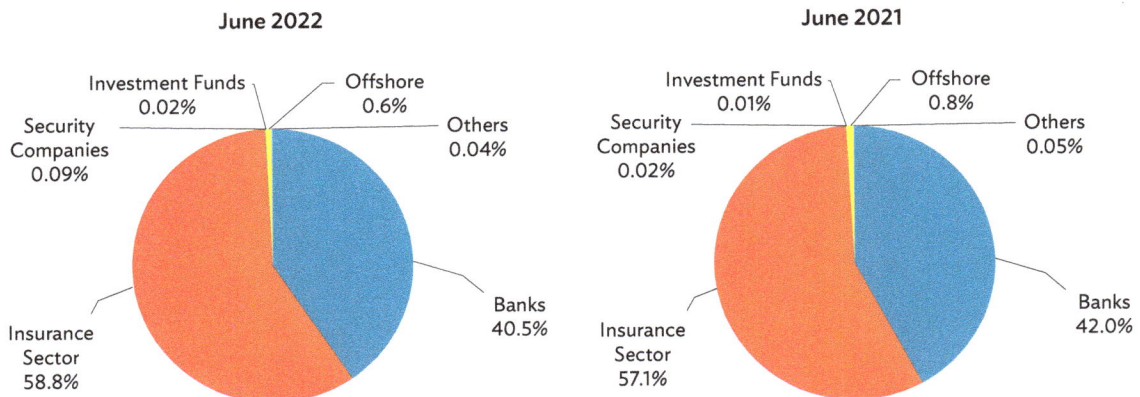

June 2022

Investment Funds 0.02%
Offshore 0.6%
Security Companies 0.09%
Others 0.04%
Banks 40.5%
Insurance Sector 58.8%

June 2021

Investment Funds 0.01%
Offshore 0.8%
Security Companies 0.02%
Others 0.05%
Banks 42.0%
Insurance Sector 57.1%

Source: Ministry of Finance, Government of Viet Nam.

Policy, Institutional, and Regulatory Developments

State Bank of Vietnam Releases Guidance for Corporates Issuing International Bonds

In July, the SBV released Circular No. 10/2022/TT-NHNN to provide guidance on foreign exchange management for corporates who issue bonds without a government guarantee in the international market. The circular provides the legal framework for borrowing and paying debt issued by corporates without guarantees. It also removed the requirement for a review of the bond issuance by a state-owned commercial bank. With the streamlined procedures, the regulation will encourage corporates to tap financing for their business operations through the issuance of international bonds.